BECAUSE I'M
Introvert
TRIUMPH

Stories on how we harness our traits
to flourish in career, business and social life

BECAUSE I'M

Introvert

TRIUMPH

Stories on how we harness our traits
to flourish in career, business and social life

Foreword By Eugene Loh

ASHLEY ELLA CHOO - RICARDO DURAN - GARY GUWE
HAZRIQ IDRUS - JUDY KOH - VERN LAI - LEE MCKING - ELIJAH LIM
KEVIN PHUN - ESTHER SIAH - FIONA TAN-LOW - MERVIN YEO

First Published May 2016
Copyright © 2016 by Internet Strategic Partners LLP

ISBN 978-981-09-8382-6

Author(s)   : Ashley Ella Choo, Ricardo Duran, Gary Guwe,
                 Hazriq Idrus, Judy Koh, Vern Lai, Lee McKing,
                 Elijah Lim, Kevin Phun, Esther Siah, Fiona Tan-Low,
                 Mervin Yeo

Publisher   : Internet Strategic Partners LLP
Cover Design   : Rizqi R. Mosmarth

http://www.BecauseIAmIntrovert.com
enquiry@BecauseIAmIntrovert.com

National Library Board, Singapore Cataloguing in Publication Data
Title: Because I'm introvert I triumph : stories on how we harness our traits to flourish in career, business, and social life.
Other title(s): Because I am introvert, I triumph | Stories on how we harness our traits to flourish in career, business, and social life
Description: [Singapore] : The Introvert Network, 2016
Identifier(s): OCN 949852189 | ISBN 978-981-09-8382-6 (paperback)
Subject(s): LCSH: Introverts. | Success.| Success in business. | Career development.
Classification: DDC 155.232--dc23

Dedicated to

Introverts Network, Singapore

and the **Introverts** who

have yet to embrace

their gifts

Contents

ACKNOWLEDGEMENTS

I want to thank all the co-authors for participating and contributing to this Introvert book project, making it a reality. It is definitely not easy for some of the authors to step up and share their personal, sometimes emotional stories. However, I'm sure their stories will change the world for the better, one introvert at a time.

I want to acknowledge Mervin Yeo for guiding us to kick-start this project, and most importantly for initiating the Introvert Network group. Because of this group, it has helped form new friendships and alliances, inspired many others to step up and to step out of their comfort zone to start networking.

Lastly, I want to acknowledge Fiona Tan-Low for putting in 101% of her heart-felt effort in managing the content and putting the pieces together. It is my privilege to work with her. Though we have encountered many challenges, it is also these challenges that make us stronger and a better person!

VERN LAI
Author and Entrepreneur

FOREWORD

Some of us were born more inward-looking - that is, we tend to search within ourselves for strength or answers, and are more likely to think more deeply on just about anything!

However, we are also more likely to feel uncomfortable or anxious when around people, especially strangers or people we don't know well. In a nutshell, we draw our energy from ourselves or from being alone in our 'space', rather than from other people or from being around them.

As a result of this, we may appear timid, passive, and slow.

We are also often made to feel inadequate or not as capable as others who are more outspoken and sociable. This happens because of the way our society conditions us to believe that 'do-ers' are better than 'thinkers' - simply because they are (by nature and as a consequence) so much more visible (not to mention audible)!

Just imagine a politician's impassioned speech.

What we see and remember is his or her powerful performance on stage. But what of the speech writer or the vocal coach, the researcher or the personal assistant who makes sure everything runs like clockwork?

Introverts possess powerful gifts that, too often and too long, have been overlooked or suppressed.

But we aren't entirely blameless - we can sometimes undermine ourselves (in the context of this society we exist in) by routinely framing our strengths as flaws or consistently remaining in the shadows.

Introverts, or people with 'introverted inclinations', will welcome the candid and illuminating personal anecdotes and reflections here.

The authors help us overcome our anxiety and misconceptions about introversion and demonstrate vividly and profoundly how it can become our greatest asset.

EUGENE LOH
Writer and Host
A Slice of Life
On 938LIVE (MediaCorp, Singapore)
Facebook, Twitter & meclub.sg

PREFACE
VERN LAI

It was late at night. Three of my friends, Mervin, Elijah and Fiona from the Introvert Networking group, braved the rain and distance to visit me at my father-in-law's wake. I shared with them, as any proud son-in-law would, about my father-in-law, who operated a small stall, "Ah Shui Pig's Stomach Soup" at Geylang Lorong 19, and about his glories in the past, his pride, a Mercedes Benz stickered full of pigs, about him being a philanthropist who was featured in newspapers and even invited onto TV shows for his expertise in his trade.

Amidst the peanuts and melon seeds cracking, and over several cups of mineral water, the conversation somehow led to a discussion about a dream unfulfilled. One of my dreams of being a published author.

The initial discussion was fruitful as Mervin is already an experienced published author of 4 books, while Fiona has always wanted to write her book too. What came out from that discussion, though still preliminary then, was the idea of a published book that would contain heart-felt stories by the Introverts from our Introvert Networking group.

Thereafter, two more meetings were all it took to finalise the direction of the book - an anthology of stories by the Introverts, to share their breakthroughs in life, be it in career, business or social context. It will be the first of a series of how Introverts triumph. It will be a book that Introverts can relate to and inspires them to embrace their Introvert traits and leverage on their traits to triumph in life…

Because I'm Introvert… I TRIUMPH!

BUTTERFLIES AND SWEATY PALMS

RICARDO DURAN

Darkness still surrounds Singapore as my phone alarm rings and wakes me up on a Friday morning at 5:30am. Yes, it is a Friday where I will be conducting a full day training event. No matter how many times I have conducted such events, every approaching session still fills me with dread. I am nervous about meeting new people. This is why I must start the day early, to psyche myself, prepare my mind and body to be as successful as I can be.

I am grateful for this nervous energy. Why? While energy untamed can be detrimental and wasted, harnessed energy can be a powerful tool if used wisely. What better way to harness this energy than to take an early morning run within the nature that is literally just minutes away from my home? Anyway, it is not like I can sleep peacefully until my normal waking up time. That never happens on a training day. Okay, now that the secret is out, I hope people do not start contacting me so early in the morning. Just kidding!

The peace in the quiet surroundings is amazing at this hour. I am comfortable in complete silence. It allows me to focus and prepare mentally for my day. I am the director of my mind, and I am slowly creating a mental movie with my thoughts on how my day will proceed. You see, I am an introvert, and one of my strengths is the ability to be thoroughly prepared.

However, this was not always a strength I knew that existed within me. How I wish I had learned this during my childhood! It would have saved me from feeling uncomfortable in huge settings or environments thronged with people I have never met. And let's not even talk about what people would think if they ever found out that I actually had to practice what I was going to say at a group gathering! Imagine the fear, not only of being in a strange environment, but also being made fun of, for preparing scripts just to talk with people. But that was exactly what I had to do. Well, we all have our own ways of preparing ourselves to face certain fears or deal with undesirable situations. We should be proud that we have the skill to do so.

Back to this Friday morning. As an introvert, I feel more in control when I understand who my audience will be and their background. That is why the day before, I had taken some time to learn more about those who are attending today's session. Where they worked, what they do now and in the past, assessed if they are at the right level for the course. More important, I am trying to put a name to a face when possible and add some human characteristics based on information I was able to gather and learn because in my mind, this is the first time I am meeting them.

During my run, I picture them coming into the classroom one by one. I am going to each individual confidently with a great smile and posture. I am not asking for their name. No, rather, I am addressing them by their name. Remember, in my movie, this is my second meeting with the attendees. Wow! Meeting them twice in a personal setting has allowed me to be more comfortable around them. Or at least that is what I thought but, as we will see shortly, that will not be the case.

For the rest of my run, I picture how I will present. This script includes my posture, the tone of my voice, the flow of the presentation and yes, the reaction of the crowd. My run is coming to an end and I feel mentally prepared as my game plan has been created. Wait, I feel doubly successful as I was able to exercise at the same time!

It is 30 minutes before the training is to start. It is still too early so nobody has arrived yet. My hands are sweaty and my gut.....is full of familiar butterflies in anticipation of people arriving shortly.

Shh... Here is a little secret. I am never able to eat breakfast or lunch on my training days! It has nothing to do with me being dedicated to the task. Nor am I on a special diet for my body to look good in front of the audience. (How I wish that was true.) No. When I eat on training days, there are so many butterflies in my stomach that they want to fly out! In other words, I feel like vomiting and, as a matter of fact, have indeed done so in the past. I know, in local slang, some people call it "Merlion", right? Have you ever had that feeling as an introvert?

It is more than just stage fright. It is a deeper conscious anxiety where logically I understand that I have done this hundreds of times but I can never avoid this feeling. The other thing I cannot avoid is going to the toilet. Speaking of which, I had better head to the toilet one final time before people start to arrive. Okay, possibly twice, but nobody needs to know the exact number.

The start of the session is getting closer. There is somebody walking towards the training room. Could it be? Yes, Yes, Yes! My first student has arrived and the mental preparation from this morning's run goes into action. Or, does it?

My old nemesis, Mr. Sweaty Palms, makes a guest appearance right on cue. Actually, he is a regular in my life. Why are my palms sweaty? I thought I was already mentally prepared???!!!

As I search for the answer, my mind starts talking to me by providing advice, "This is not the right time to start a conversation. The person will think you are strange. What if the person who just came in cannot be bothered with small talk?"

Why does this always happen to me?

Maybe my mind is right and I should avoid bothering this person. I know that these are not questions that will empower me but the voice inside my head seems so convincing. Over the years, I have learned that this is part of my script as an introvert.

In the past, I would try to overcome my hesitation with a game I like to call the 1, 2, 3 game where after 3, you would perform the action that you were afraid or hesitant to do. For example, you wanted to speak to a girl you liked but couldn't because you were too shy. 1, 2, 3, GO! Or if you wanted to participate in an interesting game but once again, you couldn't because you were too nervous. 1, 2, 3, GO! Unfortunately, I never did win in this game because I would continuously count 1, 2, 3, but never GO! 1-2-3, 1-2-3, 1-2-3, until somebody else took advantage of the opportunity and WENT.

However, now I know because I am an introvert, I can also self-reflect and provide a more empowering script for myself which I have created over the years.

My revised script is - Because I am an introvert, my Friday training always pushes me outside my comfort zone and lets me grow as a person. Training sessions will be filled with new challenges and excitement.

I start to remember my morning run and my mental preparation. It is time that I take action. I go towards the student, smiling and showing great posture. I address her by saying "Good morning, Michelle. Thank you for coming to today's training." The butterflies are now gone as my nervous anticipation has been tamed. Soon it will be time for me to present. I have overcome the first obstacle.

I may have overcome my first obstacle but have my students overcome theirs? Because I am an introvert, it is my duty to empower everyone to feel like they have a voice in my class regardless of whether they are hesitant to speak or not. In order to do that, I must create an environment where everybody feels safe. It is a safety zone where judgement and pressure are not being felt. Why not break them into smaller groups so that the audience size is not so intimidating? Why not have them speak as one team so they feel they are in it together and not afraid of being isolated?

The full day training has completed as I say goodbye to the last attendee. I am both physically and mentally drained. The truth is, at this point, I despise having any human interaction. Some may say I am moody or just being anti-social. Actually, they are right as my energy level is so low that I am not even interested in smiling. I need some alone time. As an introvert, I have been able to find creative and productive ways in creating my 'alone time'. No, it does not involve me locking myself inside a dungeon or hiding in the toilet. Rather, I will find a peaceful place to reflect on the day's events. This peaceful place is my usual favourite coffee shop where I will unwind and give myself a little reward by drinking my usual 'ice coffee' while I reflect.

Similar to how athletes may watch taped recordings of themselves to improve or strengthen their technique, I reflect on my performance for the day on where I was strong and where I could improve for the next time. Did I greet people by name? Did I transition through the slides smoothly? Was I clear and able to provide the knowledge that the students came for? Did I empower everyone in my class? Was I able to live my day similar to the movie that I created in my mind during my run?

My strength to self-reflect provides me a way to not only improve myself, but also allows me to recuperate and regain a little bit of my energy.

Would I want to do this again?

Maybe five years ago, I would say "No", because I would have focused on the end result of being drained and the anxieties that come with presenting. However, now that I focus on the process and leverage my introvert traits, the answer to this question is "Yes!"

Damn, I just remembered something very funny about myself. There was only one class in University where I got less than a B and that was Speech class. If I were to write this on WhatsApp, it would be an OMG or a LOL moment. You see, I literally stuttered and mumbled my way through the class! English is my first language, but I am sure some of my classmates thought that I was trying to learn how to speak it instead. There were times when I forgot to show my visuals which I had created. I do not want to be disgusting, but on the days I had to give a speech, I would never wear a light coloured shirt for fear that it would literally be drenched. Whether from profuse nervous perspiration, or too many Merlions, I will leave it to your imagination.

That was more than 20 years ago. Today, a more confident me looks back with amusement to see how far I have come. What a difference knowing and using my introvert traits has made.

Being an introvert and accepting who I am has allowed me to transform personally and professionally. I am grateful that I was able to find my own comfort level and understand who I am and why I may feel a certain way.

I have finally finished the last step of self-reflection which allows me to bring closure to the day. I am at peace and even though I am still exhausted, I look forward to going home and spending time with my wife and son to officially end the day. Just in time for the weekend!

I AM QUIET, I AM STRONG
KEVIN PHUN

I am a very quiet person. That is the way I have always been. For many years, people have called me introvert. Reserved. Shy. Actually, I never felt it mattered. These are all words or labels being used, but only because they have to fit me in a sentence somehow. These labels don't quite reveal who I am.

Introverts are those whom others feel are a little too quiet. However, it is not that we do not have much to say. Maybe we don't but, trust me, often times we do have things to say. We just feel that there is a better time, better place and sometimes, better things to say altogether. We just do not believe we need to express ourselves by being the loudest, or the first to break the silence, or the one who has the most things to say.

We have a fantastic awareness of what not to say during times. Even though we are usually silent, our minds are working. We watch you talk. We think about what you say, and we analyze why you said what you said.

People often don't seem to give us as much attention, because we do not create enough attention. I am often bypassed when it comes to contributing my opinions. Which is a pity, because the quiet can actually reveal so much through their silence. There is something sexy about being quiet. There are successful people whose words are few. They don't readily stand out in a crowd, simply because they speak less.

In my working life, I have always sort of envied those who seem to be able to speak out readily, those who seem to have no problems speaking to people. I struggle with speaking. There are very few times when I will start a conversation with someone, let alone engage in long conversations. I have always disliked, and still do to a certain extent, being in situations and having to talk with people whom I don't know.

You see, one of my problems is that I am extremely nervous when speaking in front of people. So I end up speaking not fluently most of the time. The other problem is that I have a speech impediment.

I have a stutter.

And so you can probably guess, I used to have a low self-esteem. There was little self-confidence in me, through my growing up and then later on, in my working years. The inability and unwillingness to speak out made me feel often that perhaps I would not amount to much.

I have had my stutter for almost 20 years. I found it so hard to speak properly. This stutter had caused me so much disappointment, anger and hurt over the years. Why me? I often felt it was a curse. At times, I fell into depression. It seemed to get worse as I grew older. I feared that the stutter would destroy my life. I was by nature, an introvert, and the stutter made me withdraw even further. I often felt like King George in the movie 'The King's Speech'.

Add to that the problem of my nerves, daily living was truly a struggle.

Even something as simple as ordering food, for example, was a huge challenge. Because certain words have letters in them that make me stutter, I would change my food orders when I could not pronounce those words. For example, I find it difficult to say the word 'orange'. So I have a problem ordering orange juice. I would look away whenever the waiter or hawker stared at me quizzically, wondering what on earth I was suffering from. Sometimes, I even get laughed at, knowingly and maybe unknowingly, for my stutter. Many times I felt depressed.

Teaching, then, sounds rather impossible.

Yet the strangest thing is, years later now, I am a lecturer by profession!

Often, when I stood in front of a class, especially in the first half before the break, I would feel nervous. Interesting thing is, I could feel this way even though I saw this group of people week in week out. The pain, when the nerves failed and I realized I could not really speak properly, was crippling. It was a mixture of anguish and disappointment. I was fearful of being seen as incompetent. This went on for some years.

Having a stutter means a lot of things in life become difficult. It was during a time, when my frustration with my speaking grew, that I sat down and really thought about what I could do about it. I knew I had to learn to manage the problem. If not, my teaching career would be impossible. Teaching is something I love doing and have been doing for 10 years.

I started to search deeper. It dawned on me. Either the problem overtakes me, or I overcome it.

I decided to take up the battle; go to war with this problem.

There are things one learns from others who have treaded through life. As I grew older, one of the best lessons I learnt is to be very good at something. One can aspire to be a photographer, but the key is to find a niche and be very good at it. One can be a cook, but it is more important to want to specialize in a particular cuisine, say, Chinese, Italian, or Thai food.

I found what I like to do when I was 30. I am a freelance lecturer, and teaching is something I love doing.

I started teaching what I know best, Tourism. And I applied the concept of self-improvement to my work; always try my best to be the best. It was not too difficult to strive to be good, as I love my work. There was this natural drive in me to be good at what I was doing.

Growing up, I had seen many people who could talk a lot, but under-performed. This made me feel that I had no reason to feel so low in self-esteem. I challenged myself to speak out and, mainly out of being sick and tired of my own 'socially timid' status, I began to be more vocal.

I started making slight changes - the way I spoke, how I should feel when I entered the classroom, and also, the things to say. I started experimenting with saying the same thing in different ways, doing little things in the class to make myself feel at ease.

I always thought not of myself but of my students, how important it was for me to get my ideas and message across to them. The quality of their education depended on the quality of my teaching, most of which was delivered by talking. I transferred the focus onto that which was more important than myself.

My eloquent thoughts were always mangled and slaughtered by shabby speech. I constantly practiced delivering the lectures. In class, I took deep breaths. I spoke slowly, more deliberately, using words that were easy on the tongue.

It was all hard work which nobody knew. Second nature to most, but it required great deliberate effort from me.

Somehow, it worked! And there were improvements.

After some time, I discovered that one of the benefits of always striving to be the best is that, not only do your skills improve, but so does your self-confidence! Mine slowly started to grow. I started to speak up more (also because I was growing older), and have less inhibitions. I was praised for my competency, and the renewed self-confidence gave me less and less reasons why I should not speak up. I gradually started teaching in bigger and more established schools, and even after I came out to lecture freelance, teaching assignments still came, by God's grace.

I became my own counsellor. I told myself that I was probably better than I thought. Why should I be afraid, when clearly I was competent in what I do? Would I gain something valuable in life, if I managed to overcome my obstacles? Were there certain skills I was not aware of, that could be found in the journey of overcoming my stutter and nervousness?

It was only when I asked these hard questions that I saw that perhaps there was some good in all these after all.

After much deep searching, I began to realize that having this stutter made me work harder. I had read that stutterers tend to be harder working than most others. That is probably true! I suspect I probably spend a bit more time than some of my peers in preparing for my lessons. I would research more, and prepare for my classes more, even for lessons I had taught for many times.

I was more perseverant. No matter how many times I saw the students, how many times I had gone over the material, I practiced. I was maybe also humbler. Instead of becoming complacent, I was encouraged with every small triumph to do better next time.

Gradually, I slowly discovered that this stutter can actually benefit me. I realized that the stutter has made me want to succeed even more, by working harder, and being more disciplined. I know that I have a deficit, and will need to work harder than the rest. I never stop. In the story of tortoise and the hare, I'm the tortoise that kept on going. This pursuit of excellence might not have been present, if I had been blessed with perfect speech.

So, when I ask, "What is the purpose of having this stutter?", somehow, I am slowly led into thinking that perhaps, the impacts of having a stutter are not always horrible, if I know how to "use" it.

When I began to see the good points about having this stutter, I no longer live with low self-esteem. The motivation to overcome my speech grew, and I found myself living my life with a greater purpose; to help others who struggle with 'obstacles' and low self-esteem.

Religion, certainly, has helped. I do believe that perhaps someone up there has a reason for me to have this stutter. I begin to trust God more and surrender my problem. I believe that 'my Lord's grace is enough for me, because his power is made perfect in weakness'. As it says in the Bible, "For I know the plans I have for you, plans to prosper you and not to harm you". Who knows? My stuttering might just be part of God's plan for me. I learn to let go and just speak, to be comfortable with my impediment.

I still have not learnt the secret to managing my nerves, or my stutter. Till today, I still feel nervous and stutter in the classroom.

But what has changed is the way I look at the issue. There is something sexy about having impediments. The journey, to understand the reasons and to overcome them, is very meaningful. Yes, there are great inconveniences when I have these two issues in my life, but the accomplishments will be doubly great.

ALONE BUT NOT LONELY
ESTHER SIAH

I did not use the name 'Esther' when I was in school. Seriously, I cannot remember how the name came about. I was Siah Yang Fern from Primary 1 all the way to Secondary 4. It was only until Junior College that I started to use the name.

Bad idea… Why? The tutors and lecturers found it easy to call me to answer questions. It's really not that I didn't know the answer. It's just that I was not comfortable with raising my hand or standing up to answer the questions. That's why I went back to Siah Yang Fern when I entered University. But, then…

Bad idea… Why?

Guys cannot remember my name!

Out of six comments in my Primary School report book, two stated, "Fair". The other four stated, "Yang Fern is a quiet girl in class".

What did that mean? What? I thought teachers liked to shout "Class, keep quiet!" So, were they the ones with the problem?

I think sometimes teachers misunderstand me or other quiet kids. There's nothing wrong with me. Plenty of people are quiet, but perfectly happy.

Is it true? Kids that talk a lot in class are usually seen as brighter, happier students by teachers? Can't be. I'm quiet as a mouse and I did quite well in most of my examinations! And I always thought the quiet ones can think deeper and concentrate better.

Oh, I hate group projects, especially so in University days. At least in secondary school or junior college, I would already have my group of 2- 3 friends where we always stuck together.

I could not find real friends in Uni days as our classes were so scattered and I saw different classmates in different subject classes.

The moment the lecturer said, "Group project, partner up," I could hear myself silently cursing in my head.

People would turn around, giving each other the eye contact, smiling and shaking hands. And I would sit there looking straight ahead hoping to catch the eye of one or two others who were like me. Then the moment came when the lecturer would throw that hateful question, "Is there anybody there that doesn't have a partner?" And I would have to drag myself to the front of the lecture hall, standing there, waiting to be adopted.

I'm a person who likes working on my own and for every project, I always believe that I'm capable of completing that on my own.

Group work was, however, something we had to go through, as learning to work with others is definitely a useful skill we will need later on in life. Thanks to the balance of individual and group work I was forced to do back then in class, I now find myself equipped with this skill.

When we learnt to identify or communicate our skills or what we were good at within the group, we harnessed our skills to the best. I always chose to do things related to designing or the creative part, perhaps setting up or decorating the room to set the mood and prepare for presentation or adding special designs to enhance presentation slides etc.

This leads me to the next thing – presentation.

If I can excuse myself from any project presentation, I'd be glad to do that. But if the criteria is that it is compulsory for all members to present, the trauma will begin weeks prior to the presentation. I'd always end up reading from my script. No eye contact, nothing, just plain reading.

When I started working, this thing worsened. I remember, when I was told to introduce myself in front of my new colleagues. Standing in front of the conference room, I could feel my cold palms and shaky legs. We had to answer two questions which had been given to us many days in advance so we could go prepare. Even so, I could hear my shaky voice and after that my manager told me that yes, it was very obvious my legs were shaking. So embarrassing!

Five years in that job, I tried many means to get out of this problem. I read all possible self-help books. I attended speech training sessions, I forced myself to attend Toastmasters. I did improve, but this was definitely not something I enjoyed doing.

Few years later, I started my own little craft business, thinking I could hide in my little workshop and keep on doing crafts all day long. But no, it does not happen that way. We can hide and produce the best items, but without any exposure or creating awareness, nobody would know.

I have to push myself to go out there and promote the items.

Remember how I hate presentations and talking to strangers? How am I going to promote my items?

In my last job, I had to force myself to go knocking on people's doors to talk to them about financial planning. I had to stand at public places and approach people, to do surveys on savings habits.

It was traumatizing and exhausting. I was trying to pass myself off as something I wasn't and it felt so wrong.

I could choose to leave that job at that time. But this time round, it's my own business, my baby. I have no choice.

I don't like pushing people, putting something in their face that they did not ask for. I prefer to be quiet and observe and let the product attract the buyer.

The strange thing is, over the years I find it getting easier to share my work with people, especially online. Every time I post something online, I get really positive comments, from friends as well as strangers. This increases my confidence and in fact it carries over offline too!

One day, I received an invitation to conduct my craft-making workshop to a group of 30 people at a community club. The butterflies started attacking my stomach again. I'm going to stand in front of people and talk. Will my legs shake? Will my voice quiver? I cannot read from script, I need to be hands-free for craft demonstration. How?

Guess what?

I aced through it! Why? Because, we were having so much fun that I did not realize how quickly the time flew by. My class actually over-ran by a whole hour. Sixty minutes!

That was just the beginning of many more craft workshops that followed. So far, the record number of craft participants is 500, can you believe that?!

The beauty of our trait – I discover I can naturally come out of my shell when I am doing something I truly love. I have a lot to say when it comes to art and the handmade marketplace.

I like to hang out alone in cafes or even hawker centres especially in the early morning. This introvert trait suits me fine because, sometimes, I just sit and stare around and sip my coffee.

Other times I will doodle and scribble in one of my many notebooks. On a good day, when creative juices start flowing, I will tear out pages and start to fold them into pieces of craft works.

I remember, I was doing this one morning in a coffeeshop near my home. One of my friends saw me and walked over to me.

"You alone? Are you alright? You want to move over to our table and join us?" She was referring to the table she was seated at with her husband.

What did she mean '*am I alright*'? Did I look so sad and pathetic to her just because I was sitting there alone? After I politely declined her invitation, she went back to her table. On and off, I looked up and I would see her giving me one of those "tender loving care" looks.

Too much distraction for me. I finished my coffee and walked away. Even though she was not sitting with me, or talking to me, I could subconsciously feel her eyes on me all the time and it was so uncomfortable.

Alone time seems to be always associated with lonely time. How shall I put this across? I'm alone but I'm not lonely. I do have friends. I do hang out with friends for coffee, meals and chit chat. It's just that I set aside more alone time for myself. I love creating and making things. I'm always alone when I create, but never lonely. In my handmade world, lots of time and work are involved in this creative journey. I don't think I can create so much if I did not have all these alone time and if I didn't enjoy solitude.

It can be rather difficult to put it across to friends that I can't go out during the whole week to meet up with them because I need to stay in my workshop to get my stuff out. It'll disrupt my thoughts and feelings.

"Not even 2 hours off? You need to eat lunch too, right?"

No, not even 2 hours off. With a 2-hour break, it'll probably take 6 hours for me to get back into the mood.

My close friends know my style. I'll set aside certain days and time to spend with them. And when I do, I make sure it's a full day, where I'm totally immersed, catching up and really listening and enjoying the moments with them. The same goes for my family members. Sundays are usually reserved for them. One full Sunday. Fair enough, right?

Someone once told me that I was 'pathetic'. Seriously! He said that, and in Mandarin, which sounded even worse! He was trying to get me to attend some business opportunity talk which happens on most of the Sunday afternoons. I told him I needed to stay at home with my kids, and he said my life was pathetic as I could not even have a Sunday to myself. Well, if that is what 'pathetic' is, then I'm perfectly fine to be pathetic!

Over the years, I read about this trait called introverts. People like to associate introverts with shy and lonely people. I guess it's because the world is such that they favor extroverts. Friendly, humorous, loud and outgoing people. Don't we remember who the popular girls are in school? The guys always remember them and want to hang out with them, while we are hiding in a corner sometimes secretly wishing we are like them, going up the stage, telling jokes, singing songs so naturally. We are introverts living in an extrovert world, sometimes we feel an imbalance.

I've been reading up on the subject and I now understand the trait better. Understanding and acknowledging makes me feel so happy. I can accept the true me and use this trait to my advantage. My way to shine is by excelling in my handcrafting world.

I do not fall prey to the idea that I must be out-going, or constantly networking, or collaborating to get ahead. I have within me a different, but important, skill set. I use my inborn talents and tendencies to solve problems for the world and in that way, I will remain my authentic self.

I thoroughly believe it's good to push myself out of my comfort zone, but I don't believe it is right to punish myself for the way I was born. Then again, sometimes I do remind myself I should not use this as an excuse for staying within my comfort zone.

"I know the answer, I don't raise my hand

I sit in a café by myself, I don't have a problem

I'm alone, I'm not lonely ...

I think, I read, I create, I make ...

The most wonderful stuffs

My name is Esther..."

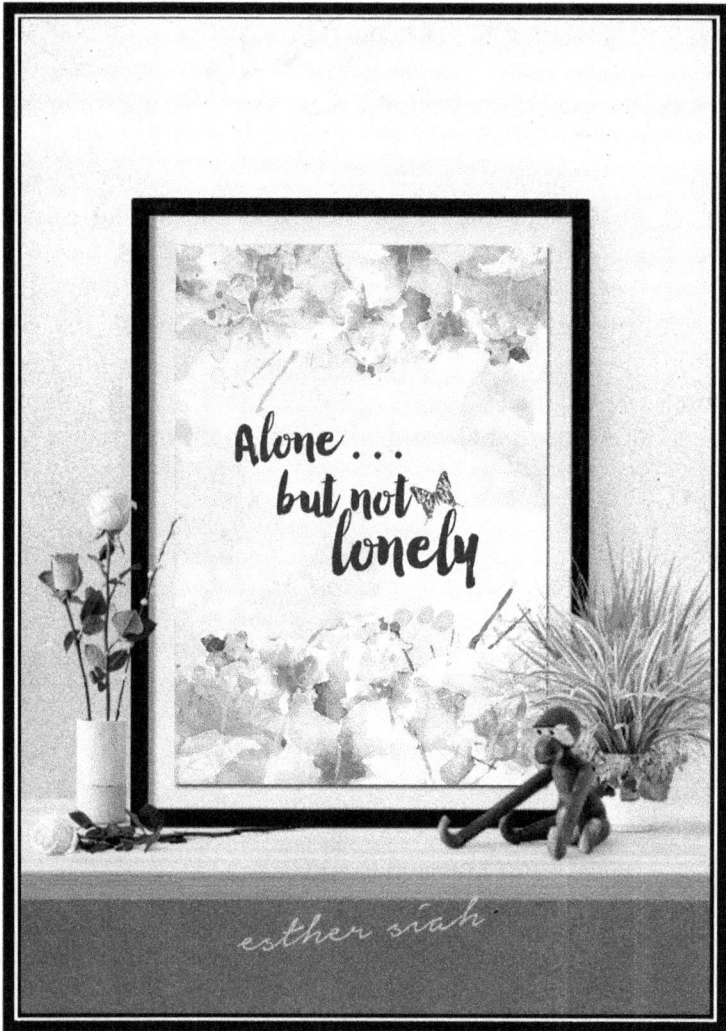

Alone . . .
but not
lonely

esther siah

THE INFLUENTIAL INTROVERT
GARY GUWE

It was 3pm, on a regular Friday afternoon. The appointment had been set with Shaun, the new Vice-President of Sales from a company I was previously engaged with. Waltzing into the office, I was fully expecting a casual and comfortable conversation to see how he was fitting in his new role, and also to pick his brain on leadership for a new book I'm coming up with on the Authoritative Art of Influence.

Swooping through the office, I said my hellos to a number of ex-colleagues, whatever few that I still knew since I left the company two years ago. I was 'caught' and quickly pulled into the office by my friend, Wendy, the HR Manager with whom I had worked closely, when we had the same boss.

"Gary, I'm sorry for this! We have leadership team from the Global Training Office here today, and our regular trainer is going on maternity leave in a couple of weeks. We would like you to consider returning to the company and take on your old role, albeit as an external contractor on an interim basis. They'll be meeting you in 10 minutes", she quipped.

"Did she just set me up for an interview with the leaders of this company...?" were the sub-titles screaming in bold fonts (and underlined in italics) at the back of my head.

"I know it's really last minute, but they mentioned earlier today that they were looking for somebody dynamic and a person who cares enough about the growth of people to go the extra mile... that's when I thought of you and put your name forward! It's by divine appointment that you'd scheduled an appointment to meet with

Shaun today as well! Will you just go into the meeting with them and see how it goes?" she continued.

"Sounds interesting…," was the response I gave. In fact, that's the default response I give in response to most if not all developments, requests and impromptu events in my life, regardless of whether they're good or bad.

So just like that, I entered the boardroom, where I'd spent so many days presenting proposals and updates to leaders and directors of a company I'd left over two years ago. Just like that, this introvert went for an impromptu interview, with two Americans who flew halfway around the world to revolutionize the Learning and Development department vision, mission and execution of a NASDAQ-listed company that, some observers felt, have lost their way. Just like that, this 'quiet' introvert survived a half-hour, unplanned sharing session with two corporate leaders, with very exacting standards, who spoke of their grand plans for the company. Just like that… this introvert was offered a job, on the spot!

One might be tempted to feel that the manner this entire episode unfolded might come across as frivolous and unprofessional. Perhaps, more care, planning and preparation could've been in place before the leaders reached out to me. I was impressed though, that the two Americans had already spoken with other local and senior leaders of the company who'd the experience of working with me previously, and had gone as far as looking through my documents and remuneration package from yester-years. The men had done their homework, and the impromptu interview was scheduled to suss me out - to see if I was the real deal.

In their own words, "We've heard a lot about you; and the questions you've brought up during our conversation have given us a pretty good confirmation of what we have heard. We're looking for people who care about the development of our people here… and your coming back to follow up with and checking up on your old friends here, when you didn't need to, speaks volumes of your character and personality. We do hope that we can work together."

My response to them went along the lines of, "In all honesty, I did swing by to have a cuppa coffee!"

We had a laugh, and we left it at that. I promised them that I'd get back to them within a week with my interest and response.

The story I shared was a true story that happened in late April 2016.

The Journey So Far

It was remarkable, not merely because of how suddenly things developed, but because of how far I've developed as an individual, since I embarked on my journey of personal development, awareness and acceptance of myself as an introvert, from 11 years ago.

In this time, I've co-founded three businesses, been appointed lecturer to post-graduate students at the National University of Singapore and undergrads at the ESSEC Business School, and headhunted by an American MNC. I've also served twice as President of the NUS Toastmasters Club, and I have been interviewed by local radio and international publications on issues pertaining to communication, public speaking and confidence.

Till date, I'm a professional coach, speaker and trainer who specialises in the Authoritative Art of Influence. I teach individuals how to reach out to people, connect with customers, speak confidently, present persuasively and close more sales. I even count speakers, lecturers and experienced sales people in my profile of students!

Over the course of my career, I've spoken to over 17,000 individuals from around the world. Not bad, for a person who prefers to be found at the back of a room, seated in a corner, by himself.

Actually, given the choice I'd probably prefer not to be found at all! Give me my peace and give me my space; meeting new people and having conversations tire me out. I don't hate people; my energy is merely discharged and recharged differently.

Anyway, I digress.

Not Always Conversant

I wasn't always conversant. I wasn't always confident. Even on some days now, I've felt that I'm incompetent. But I've certainly come a long way from the days of being that 'shy introvert' who dared not speak up, and the one who preferred to reserve his best thoughts and ideas in the depths of his mind.

"It'll be too much trouble...", "not worth the time...", "not worth the effort", "too tiring to try...", "I can't speak as well...", "I'll let somebody else say it..." – these were some of the repeated phrases that came up over the course of my life.

Somehow, for so many of the ideas that I had, I never really found the courage to share them and help them see the light of day, during the first 20 years of my life.

I've always been thoughtful and analytical. I realized that I was pretty introspective and preferred to reflect on events and experiences I went through to derive meaning and learning lessons I could apply. I developed many theories about how things worked, and how they should work. Sadly, I never had the opportunity to test them out and bring to life.

A large part of that was due to a lack of courage and fear of failure. Another huge part of that reluctance to share those ideas and try them out, was a lack of competence in the ability to communicate those ideas and win support for them.

The First Signs of Strengths

Still, the first, and probably the only time I found myself passionate enough to put my ideas and theories into practice, came when I was sixteen. Then, I was serving as student leader in charge of a group who were two years my junior.

I vividly recall, as one of the youngest groups of students who'd signed up for the National Cadet Corps (Land) unit, my juniors were frequently chided and ridiculed for their poor performance and lack of discipline in the eyes of their peers... and even our teachers. There was hardly a morning that went by, without my discipline master making a snide comment about a boy from my group.

Through my initial interactions and observations, I quickly realized that the reason for their poor performance stemmed from poor guidance and lack of structured instruction from my predecessor who'd squandered away the time he had for training them. A new development plan was drawn up in a week, and over the course of a year, we witnessed a massive transformation of over 20 young gentlemen - myself included.

My work as a sixteen-year-old, with a group of teenaged boys who were two years younger than me, was the first indication of my strengths and analytical abilities - borne out of introspection, observation and ability to hold conversations and listen.

Where most people in my position (at that point in time) would scream and shout as 'leaders' in military fatigue, I balanced my approach with understanding and education through conversations with each and every individual in my platoon. To the best of my knowledge, nobody else had ever done something like that before, and I was proud, albeit pleasantly surprised by the results we achieved at the end of one year.

My 'boys' began as the joke of the school. By the time I was done, so reliable had they become, that they were the school and teachers' go-to guys for events set-up and preparation. They were fifteen years old, and truly the school's new student leaders.

Embracing My Strengths and Who I Am

Over the course of my life and career so far, I've begun to realize several traits and insights about 'being introverted'. Indeed, to many, we could come across as aloof, sometimes awkward, or even unfriendly or intimidating. Like many, I've once regarded these as weaknesses or limitations, things I wished I never had to put up with.

Yet, I've come to realize that our 'reservations' around people are also largely borne out of our preference and inclination for introspection, quality relationships and conversations with people. Our abilities to 'keep quiet' and listen, to pick up non-verbal cues and emotions... ironically, provide us with the pre-requisite traits to hold real quality conversations! Truly, no two people can speak at the same time - there needs to be a listener and a speaker at any point in time.

That realization that my perceived 'limitations' were actually potential strengths in disguise, changed the way I saw myself, and also surfaced areas for development.

I began applying my analytical abilities to learning and picking up the art and craft of public speaking, leadership, relationships and impromptu speaking.

As I observed what made people tick, I began applying the principles, tools and strategies in my career, business and achieved more than what many of my peers have achieved in the same amount of time.

That's not to say that I've 'made it'. Far from it.

Yet, what I've truly discovered is a deeper sense of peace and fulfilment in who I am, what I've got, and what I have to give to others, regardless of whether they're fourteen years old in school, or forty and fighting in the marketplace.

I have embraced my introversion and used it to push the envelope. I've ventured beyond my comfort zone in search of tools, principles and strategies that work and have shared them with enough people to see that they've worked for others too.

I sincerely believe that everybody, introverts included, has a gift that can be used to empower and inspire the world... and I truly hope that we can all find the courage and call to explore, and discover and become a blessing to the world.

PUSH FACTOR TO ACHIEVING
MERVIN YEO

In August 2015, at a family gathering on National Day, my daughter asked her older cousins if they could recite the pledge. No one wanted to start. The reason was simple! No one could recall. I could not help feeling amused to see them struggle to complete what they started.

It's a sad truth but I think many Singaporeans do not remember the pledge or National Anthem. When one of my nephews saw me shake my head in dismay, he challenged me to try. I took up his challenge. To their surprise, I recited the pledge, from start to end without missing a single word, "We, the citizens of Singapore, pledge ourselves... so as to achieve happiness, prosperity and progress for our nation."

They Made Me Do It

Many will be surprised that I managed to pull that off. I'm going to tell you a little secret.

Many moons ago, at eleven years of age (Primary 5), I had the unenviable task of leading the school to recite the pledge every morning of the week for almost a year. To this day, I wonder how someone, who hated to be on stage, could stand before 800 students and teachers. For the record, I did not enjoy the attention! No way! I felt uneasy and nervous having so many pairs of eyes staring at me! A scary thought just recalling!

During that year, I would always blame the ones who made me do it. My form teacher, who doted on me because I was a good student, had recommended me to the Vice-Principal to lead the school in the pledge! I was upset with both of them.

If you are an introvert, you will probably understand my sentiments. It is considered normal for people to fear public speaking; for us introverts, it is worse than the fear of death. In retrospect, I am now thankful, for the opportunity given to me was actually the stepping stone to opportunities to speak, teach and train people in different settings - halls, theatres, classrooms and even online. What the teachers did all those years ago, had paved the way for my career several decades later.

Doing What Comes Not So Naturally

Articles, books and experts tell us that networking is useful for job recommendations, to generate business referrals and for interacting with people. Whether one is a business owner, sales executive or manager, it pays to network and it pays really well to network effectively. One can never know when an opportunity may knock on the door, and one never knows when the need may arise to leverage on the expertise of someone else to get things done in one's organisation.

I have been in the networking arena for well over 15 years. That requires me to meet and interact with people all the time – from small meetings of 15 to larger events like conferences with 600 attendees. Truth be told, I still feel overwhelmed and even stressed in social settings like networking meetings and events.

Generally, I do not like to socialise, but I have discovered that when I began to value the benefits of networking, I made every effort to make networking work for myself. Picking up skills through reading and training, I started to appreciate quality relationships with others. I had moved on from gaining the knowledge to passing on the knowledge – through my own articles, books, talks as well as training and workshops.

After many years of doing this, I have, to a large extent, overcome my social awkwardness, but I am certain I have not transformed into an extroverted being. Most definitely not! My core introversion remains, I just relate better.

Like any other business skills, networking is a skill that requires time to practice. As one accumulates experience by attending networking meetings, one becomes better at it and to the point of feeling confident in interacting with people, regardless of their designations or fields of expertise.

Leadership Beckons

During my tenure as the Singapore national director of an international business networking organization operating in over 50 countries, I saw millions of dollars pass among the members. It was a powerful platform but it took a lot out of me in more ways than one. Besides the workload and leadership responsibilities, it was the requirement of being a public face that was toughest to cope with.

At one of the breakfast meetings, a lawyer teasingly addressed me as the 'poster-boy' of the organization. I did not like what he said. I did not enjoy being a recognizable face at all. I have refused time and again to have my photo inserted on my name card. I shy away from photographers and videographers. I hate posing for them.

The position of leadership required me to be known by the members and understandably so. As business professionals who pay membership fees, it was important for them to know the leader they are following.

Like networking, it was mostly on the job training for my role as a leader. As someone who disliked stage lights beaming upon my face, I survived 13 years in an uncomfortable role, by staying true to myself. I had a simple objective of wanting local business owners to do better.

Authenticity has always been a guiding trait that enabled me to lead.

As a leader, I had to maintain a positive attitude, work outside my comfort zone, and reach out to people of diverse professions and trades. There was a need, and I stepped up, despite my unspoken fears and initial reluctance.

Better Business Connections

Besides looking back, looking within will reveal that by tapping positively into my inherent traits, I was able to more than get by in the business world.

1. Listen Well

Although my work requires me to speak frequently, I would much rather listen than speak. If I do not have anything meaningful to say, I prefer to keep mum. That makes me very observant, so I am able to pick up details about people and about what they say. I make mental notes and find ways to help the person in future. This trait enables me to decide if there is a business connection. It positions me well to consider whether or not to do business with the new acquaintance.

2. Value Quality Relationships

During networking meetings and events, I do not go around passing my business cards as if they were promotional flyers. My name cards are precious; I exchange them with a handful of individuals whom I have had conversations with. I am more concerned about fostering connections than self-promotion. For those on the receiving end, it means that I pay attention to what is important to them, and I work hard to forge strong relationships. This also indicates that any business connection I make will be long-lasting. Numbers are not the way I relate with people. Alignment is.

3. Enjoy Discussing Ideas

I do not get a thrill of engaging in small talks. However, when I have an idea worth exploring, and one that is aligned to my personal goals, I will not hold back my enthusiasm. If anybody needs to brainstorm ideas for a new business venture, I can be counted on to tap into my creative juices to help, if asked. I tend to see the bigger picture, so when people work with me, they will notice how focused I can be on the larger goal of the collaboration or partnership.

Quietly Noticeable

I find it troubling each time I hear of introverts who believe that their introversion is some kind of character flaw. Thinking this way has a negative effect on the career track of the individual. Imagine my horror when someone replied me this way: "Yes Mervin, I'm an introvert but I wish I wasn't."

WHAT?!!

Let me be crystal clear! There is absolutely nothing wrong being introverted.

Since this is part of your personality that cannot change, why not embrace it and use it to your advantage? Being able to listen helps introverts to pick out ways in which they can potentially add value to someone they come into contact with. Introvert or not, you should be aware of your strengths, competencies and special skills. You could, and should, find your own unique way of communicating and connecting with others.

Over the years, I have learnt to embrace my introversion. I have built scores of meaningful and profitable connections with people in the marketplace. I stop allowing my introversion to hold me back from achieving what I set out to do. The ability to connect means that I can avail myself to do good work in the community.

When asked a question in a meeting, and I know the answer but feel awkward to raise my hand in front of everyone, I can choose to tell the person privately. If I want to volunteer for charitable service, I simply have to approach the person in charge.

It's up to me. I now choose what works for me.

Life at work as well as the community has become more fulfilling for all concerned. Everybody gains! And the wonderful thing is to know that my personality no longer stands in the way of great things being achieved.

AND I THOUGHT I WAS AN EXTROVERT!
ELIJAH LIM

The tea was icy cold. Dancing eddies swirled madly about in front of my chest before disappearing to my left in the slowly gathering dawn. Others tugged at my ALICE[1] pack, urging me to join them in their merry dance downstream. Not an invitation I'd accept with any relish. Then my feet started to move upwards and before long, I was making the safety rope fast on the far bank of what had been an ankle-deep stream just the evening before. A bit of tropical rain in the distant hills had certainly made a lot of difference.

Turning about, I gave the signal that the safety rope was in place, and the troops started to cross, their snap links connecting them to the submerged ribbon that would ensure they did not get swept away. We waited until everyone was safely across, pulled the last Instructor over with the safety rope, and continued on our way. The way Introverts do. Without fanfare, no fuss, just do what needed to be done, and brew our own cups of tea after the troops were bedded down for the night. And I thought I was an Extrovert!

Introversion and Extraversion meant nothing to me before the mid-1990s. I wasn't even aware that those terms existed! It was only during the last ten years of my active service with the Armed Forces that "soft skills", with their multitude of terms, started to make themselves known. For me, at least. I wasn't too bothered, I had more than enough to do as it was. Even after I left the Forces in 2005, I didn't really get a sufficient grasp of what they really were until perhaps 2010. Even then, I still thought I was an Extrovert. The fact that I **wasn't** an Extrovert didn't hit me until perhaps around 2012-2013.

---

[1] **ALICE**: All-purpose Lightweight Individual Carrying Equipment

Why did I think I was an Extrovert?

Well, that was partly due to DISC[2] parlance. I was introduced to DISC around 2006 and did the assessment, which proclaimed me to be a **D-I-C**. **D-I-C** meant Dominance-Influence-Compliance, and that meant that I was an Extrovert! Or did it? I've been mulling over this since the year 2013 or so, when my friend Mervin Yeo included me in a networking group for Introverts on Facebook. I didn't have any "Eureka!" moments; the realization that I was, indeed, actually an Introvert sort of grew on me slowly. Quite Introvertish, come to think of it.

Allow me to explain a little. The chart you see below summarizes the behavioural tendencies of the four traits.

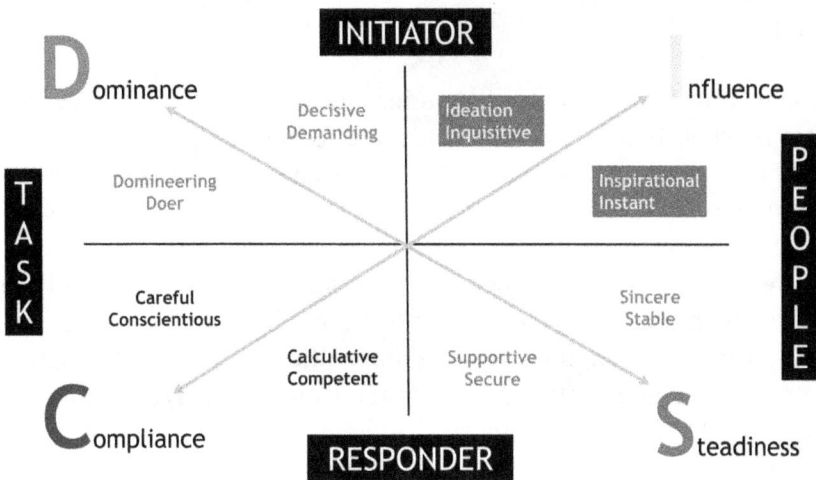

INITIATOR

Dominance   **I**nfluence

Decisive   Ideation
Demanding   Inquisitive

Domineering   Inspirational
Doer   Instant

T A S K

Careful   Sincere
Conscientious   Stable

Calculative   Supportive
Competent   Secure

Compliance   **RESPONDER**   **S**teadiness

P E O P L E

The diagonal arrows reflect the fact that people with strong **D** traits would tend to have lower **S** traits and vice versa. The same thing happens for the **I** and **C** traits. People with stronger **D** and **I** traits

---

[2]**DISC**: Dominance, Influence, Steadiness, Compliance. A psychometric framework based on the work of William Marston, circa 1928. **D** and **I** have a degree of equivalence to Extraversion, and **S** and **C** to Introversion.

35

are deemed to be more active, falling under the "Extrovert" side of the fence. Those with stronger **S** and **C** traits are deemed to be more passive, or responsive, than active, thus falling under the "Introvert" side. **D** and **C** tend to be more concerned about completion of tasks, while **I** and **S** tend to be more concerned about people and relationships.

Since my assessment showed me as being a **D-I-C**, I automatically became an Extrovert because I was more **D** and **I** rather than **C**, **C** and **S** commonly being associated with Introversion.

However, after seeing many hundreds, perhaps thousands, of DISC reports and talking to their respective owners, I have come to realize that such correlations are roughly there, but they do not describe everything there is to know. Yes, people in general do realize that, too.

The trouble is, the more we brandish such terms, the more we think that is what defines us as persons. We forget that all such terms, as they are used in the psychometric world, are snapshots, and not the whole person!

Moreover, the DISC framework is based on the work of William Marston, modelled after the theories of Hippocrates, where D ~ Choleric, I ~ Sanguine, S ~ Phlegmatic and C ~ Melancholy. Introversion and Extraversion come from the MBTI framework developed by Myers-Briggs and modelled after Jungian theories.

Yes, as I shall illustrate, I **am** a **D-I-C**, but I am **also** an Introvert. And I thought I was an Extrovert!

Casting my mind back to how I have tended to respond to others, especially in the course of, first, professional, and then, business transactions, I realize that much of my perceived Extraversion could be attributed to my highly energetic, professional and persistently enthusiastic manner. However, that seemingly bubbly exterior was over an extremely cold and formal determination to carry out a mission. In the Armed Forces, my mission was to train and prepare men for combat. Period. Everything else was either secondary or of no importance at all. It was one of the reasons why I never took up distractions like golf and absolutely loathed forced productivity measures like Work Improvement Teams (WITs).

It was also one of the reasons why I never bothered with promotions. Let me give you an example.

In 1998, I was on a six-month upgrading course. At that time, I was a Rifle Company Trainer and I enjoyed that job immensely. Returning to my office to pick something up one evening, I happened to bump into my stand-in, whom I shall call "52". "52" told me that he had heard that I was scheduled to be posted to Headquarters after the course, and that his source was reliable. I knew "52" long enough to know that what he had said was true, and a hollow, sick feeling came over me. I loved my current appointment and had absolutely no desire to be posted anywhere, least of all to Headquarters. I knew that I would hate whatever appointment I would be given, and I wondered whether I could get myself out of this predicament.

So I arranged for an interview with the Big Boss, whom I shall call "Shanghai Noon." Now, this was happening at the time of the year when promotions either took place, or didn't, and for me it happened to be the latter. I had actually been ranked high enough to have been promoted that year, but circumstances dictated otherwise. Not that I cared. I had something else in mind.

"Come in, let me explain to you why you were not promoted", Shanghai Noon said when I walked into his office.

"That's not why I'm here, Sir" I responded.

"Oh? Then why did you ask to see me?" he asked.

"I heard I'm to be posted to HQ after the course, Sir. Is that true?"

"Why, yes", he replied, "It's a good posting for you."

I immediately responded "Request to remain in current post, Sir."

Well, the long and short of it is that my request to remain in my current appointment was "duly noted", which of course meant a simple "No."

I made no other attempt to change things. You would have expected an Extrovert to have tried to wrangle his way through, right? Although I didn't know whether or not I was supposed to be an Extrovert or Introvert at the time, the frameworks also say that we are hard-wired to be one way or the other.

So, having in 2006 been classified by the DISC framework as leaning towards Extroversion, it meant that I was largely "Born that way." Really? An Extrovert would have been good at arguing his case. Not me. Yes, I was, and probably still am, a **D-I-C**. But an Introverted **D-I-C**.

Well, an Introverted **D-I-C** might not have wrangled his way out of situations he didn't like very much, but quite a few Bosses certainly found him pretty useful!

I had a reputation for bringing order out of chaos. One or two Bosses said of me quite openly "He doesn't give trouble." One chap who happened to take over one of my operations appointments kept calling me for a few months after I'd handed over, asking me about this, that and the other.

"How on earth do you manage to remember these things?" he asked in exasperation one day, after I'd explained how the calendar was actually filled in. I didn't think there was anything to it. Introverted **D-I-C**s do get things done. Quietly. Just don't push them too far.

I remember being on maybe six committees at one point. Ok, I exaggerate, but it was definitely too many. Since I believed with all my heart that all committees did were keep a lot of minutes and waste many hours, and with good reason, I loathed the enormous waste of time that represented.

One day, I happened to get summoned to attend a last-minute meeting. My request to be excused because I was in the middle of another work project was of course "duly noted." However, on this particular day I had had enough. Calling one of the clerks to me, I asked him to take some masking tape and make it look as though that was all that was holding me together. Having been thus decorated, I went down to the conference room for the meeting.

The Chairman looked at me with a why-does-it-have-to-be-me sort of look and said "Ok, you can go."

I didn't wait to be told twice. Introverted **D-I-C**s find ways to put their point across.

After I left the Forces, I sold land investments for a while. I was very good at keeping clients updated as to how the land parcels were progressing vis-à-vis their re-zoning, which would of course have increased their value. Not content with information provided by the company, I used Google Earth photos of the land parcels to show how adjacent suburban development was getting closer and how developers would be negotiating to buy the land. A photo, like that shown in next page, would be superimposed on maps given by the company so that clients would get a better picture of how their land parcels were doing.

But I was not good at getting more new clients. I thought that, being an Extrovert, I should be able to sell quite naturally. Well, I did, but I could only sell to certain categories of clients, those that I developed a relationship with first. Did I apply the sales techniques

I was taught? You bet. Was I getting sales? Not quite. You see, I was an Introvert trying to sell like an Extrovert.

I've come quite a long way since. Having gradually discerned that I'm actually an Introvert, I've developed my own way of doing business. Introverts like me tend to go for the relationship first, so sales volume would seem low at the start. However, sales volume would pick up as time goes on and relationships with clients are maintained. In fact, business volume would grow by leaps and bounds simply because all of us, whether Introverts or Extroverts, like to do business with people we like. However, that's not what the sales gurus are, or at least, were, telling you.

The common misconception people get is that Extroverts make better salespersons because of how they are wired. So, Introverts try to act like Extrovert salespersons, and guess what? They fail, at least initially. Many Introverts don't seem to succeed in sales because they don't play to their own innate strengths. When they do, business volume starts to go up.

In a world that exalts Extroversion, I'm glad I've finally discovered my own, quiet, unique, Introvert strengths. Actually, I've been playing to my own strengths all my life, except for when I was starting in business. No one told me for the longest time. Then I was given the wrong impression of myself, which lasted for a while.

But now I know. I hope you know, too. Takes a lot of stress out of trying to fit into a mould you were never designed for.

HOW I BECAME A HYPNOTIST
LEE MCKING

Hi! My name is Lee McKing and I am a hypnotist. You might be curious about my name so I will quickly share. My dad idolised Steve McQueen, who was a famous actor during the time of Bruce Lee (in fact, they were friends!) and decided the firstborn shall be named after him. And since I am a guy, therefore my name is McKing. In addition, the Chinese tradition is to have the family name in front, hence my full name is Lee McKing.

And in case you are wondering, no I don't have a sister, and I have two younger brothers. Also, yes, my name has been teased and abused even up until today. But we are not talking about that now.

For the longest time, I've known I am an introvert. And some of my traits showed their strongest growth when I started playing Chinese Chess after my PSLE.

Back then, I knew nothing of Chinese Chess. Exams were over and school became a place to have fun and relax. A great friend of mine was bored one day and asked if I knew how to play Chinese Chess. I didn't and so, he taught me. I love learning new things so I absorbed rather quickly. The names of the pieces, the movements and the rules of the game. Finally, we started playing and naturally, I lost my first game. However, I kept winning after.

You see, I could analyse the game and how he played in order to learn from it and play those strategies in later games. It's like having the ability of adaptability and evolution of the liquid metal terminator.

I was not only learning in the game, but improving on my mental processes as well. A quick look into my thought process is that for every move my opponent makes, I will think of a minimum of three counter moves and five steps into each move. That's like having three mini game plans and developing the foresight into the game.

Naturally, I enjoyed myself very much, not so much in winning, but in learning new things.

A couple of classmates noticed my "winning streak" and one of them said, "McKing, Chinese Chess is about losing. Come, let me show you how to lose!" and we started playing.

Fortunately, I had honed my abilities to a sufficient level to analyse and adapt within the game itself. And because I kept winning, his conditions increased from "best 2 out of 3" to "best 6 out of 11".

I didn't realize it then, but there was actually a hierarchy of Chinese Chess ranks within the class. Hence, the next better player would challenge me after realizing the current challenger could not teach me "how to lose". I was suddenly thrust into the competitive world of Chinese Chess – kid style.

Gradually, more and more onlookers watched the games that I was playing as I won challenge after challenge. Some were impressed at how I was winning. Others grew jealous of such skill. So far, it was the discovery of a hidden talent for me, and a whole new world of fun!

As I rose up the ranks and played against the better players, eventually, I caught the attention of the Chinese Chess King or "Qi Wang" of the class. He had a history of being trained by his father and brother since young and no one in the class could beat him. When I looked over at him in his corner, it was like watching a God of Gamblers movie, where the main character sat surrounded by his loyal supporters, his right hand man by his side.

The game between the "Qi Wang" and myself was scheduled for the day after. Apparently, he only played a certain number of games each day and that day was reaching its end.

Was I anxious? Was I afraid? Actually, I wasn't. I just wanted to have fun, to learn and analyse the game for self-improvement. Also, it was exciting to discover and grow my newly discovered talent. The growing anticipation within my chest kept me up longer that night.

When the time came, I was escorted to his table. The Chinese Chess set was already set up and the "Qi Wang" cast a glance at me while enjoying a shoulder massage by his right hand man. I wondered what that look meant. I smiled as he raised his right hand to stop the massage. We began playing.

A crowd gathered to watch. Halfway through, the crowd of onlookers released a huge gasp! "Qi Wang" turned pale as his jaw dropped. Honestly, I had no idea how to see a winning game yet so I was a bit confused when they claimed it was just a practice session and had to restart the match. So we restarted but it wasn't long before "Qi Wang" collapsed in his chair in defeat, his face in complete shock. The crowd fell silent.

"We have a new Qi Wang..." someone murmured in astonishment.

Since then, these traits have allowed me lots of growth in various situations, like when I learnt Neurolinguistic Programming or NLP and hypnosis. Before I go into how I use my analytical skills in learning NLP and hypnosis, let me share a bit about how I got interested in it in the first place.

You see, when I was 20 years old, I nearly died in my sleep.

My lung burst.

Back then, I was a first-year student in polytechnic, and it was the last week on the first term of school. I woke up that Tuesday morning and found myself having difficulty breathing. I had a presentation to give, so I had to go to school.

However, my breathing difficulties escalated. Even my speech was affected. This is because we require air when we talk, so as my breathing difficulties increased, my ability to speak in longer sentences reduced.

Needless to say, I had to cut my presentation short by almost half.

By this time, I was in pain too. It was as if every step I took brought pain to my back. It felt like someone took a knife and stabbed me there, and periodically sent electric shocks into my body through the knife. This was when I decided to go to the doctor.

Even the bus journey to the nearby doctor hurt. Fortunately, two of my classmates accompanied me and reassured that I was going to be okay although, by the looks of their faces, I probably didn't look so good.

When we reached the GP clinic, it was another painstakingly long time (well, maybe it was much shorter but it felt like eternity) before I got to see him. After listening to my description of the morning and listening to my lungs with his stethoscope, the doctor said, "Go straight to A&E, don't go home understand? Go straight to A&E now. Do you want me to call an ambulance?"

Wait, what? An ambulance?? Erm no, I think I will just get a taxi there...

At this time, thoughts were flooding into my mind... was my lung filling up with water? Internal bleeding? What the hell is happening??

When we reached the A&E, I thanked my classmates and told them to go back to school. Partly because they only allowed one visitor to accompany me, and partly because studies are important.

They took an X-ray of my chest and put me in a wheelchair with a blanket. Hmm…

Finally I entered the A&E proper and one of the doctors there showed me my X-ray.

My lung had collapsed to about a couple inches size!!!! WHAT A SHOCK!!!

"You will die…" the doctor announced.

I collapsed to the ground crying. My life flashed before my eyes.

You could even say I was in hysteria!

I had a lot of regrets because I wasn't even 21 yet! From studies, to family, from relationships to experiencing life! I thought, I haven't even truly lived yet!!!!

Meanwhile the doctor was continuing his explanation of what could happen to me in this state where my right lung had collapsed to such a size.

A pause in the story for a moment, because this is important.

You see, quite by accident, the doctor accidentally hypnotised me.

In hypnosis, there is something known as a shock induction, where the hypnotist shocks the subject and says, "Sleep!" and the subject goes into hypnosis. What the doctor did was similar, when he shocked me with the X-ray and said, "You will die…"

In addition, my unconscious mind absorbs everything without criticising, so it linked doing a presentation and after a presentation, have a near-death experience. As a result, I developed Post Traumatic Stress Disorder or PTSD for short, and with links to presentations.

A quick overview of what happened the next two and a half years in polytechnic. You can imagine how many presentations there were. Every single presentation, I had to run to the toilet (or somewhere private) where I could collapse to the ground (usually I would lean and collapse onto the sink), and I would lose control of my body.

My tears would flow, my mucus would flow. I even had salivation! Feelings of dread and fear seeped into my bones. Grief and sadness and so much more. I could barely stand and sometimes I actually vomited (more often it was just nausea). I would look in the mirror, just wondering to myself… since when did I have such severe stage fright?

Little did I know, it was actually PTSD. The traumatic near-death experience was associated with completing a presentation.

It's like a fear of cats. You see a cat, and you feel fear. In my case, I would complete a presentation, and I would be overcome with all the feelings associated with having a near-death experience.

Anyway, you may or may not know this, but the mind and body are connected. So with each presentation I completed in polytechnic, my mind would "die" due to the PTSD, and my body would "die" a bit with it.

To the extent where I was deathly pale and my fingernails were dark purple. People thought I was a sickly person even though I didn't actually fall sick.

It wasn't until after graduation from polytechnic that I wanted to get my health back in order. That was when a Facebook ad about NLP having holistic techniques to help in improving health and healing popped up on my Facebook feed.

After doing a bit of research, I decided to take up NLP from an Australian school.

Now when I was learning NLP, I readily absorbed and adapted the techniques and knowledge. My mind was like a firecracker with the energy of nuclear fission. It grew and expanded and improved as I reprogrammed my mind. Understanding the human mind never amazed me as much until now.

After attending the Master NLP Practitioner class, I realized the core techniques of NLP was from hypnosis. That was when I decided to educate myself on hypnosis and hypnotherapy. Attending the first course on hypnotherapy brought me to new unexplored places in my mind.

Bringing both skillsets of NLP and hypnotherapy together required my analytical skills and allowed me to modify some of the techniques to make them more effective. Especially with the understanding that everyone is different and there isn't any one-size-fits-all technique.

I used all my knowledge to help myself first and foremost, to grow even more as an individual and to resolve some of my other issues like the PTSD and fear of public speaking. It wasn't until I helped my mum to heal her swollen arm that I began to consider setting up my own hypnotherapy practice.

My mum is rather short and one day at NTUC, she reached to the highest shelf to take some detergent and injured her wrist. Her arm began to swell until it was three times its size! It was very painful for her but she endured the pain.

My youngest brother and I tried to convince her to allow me to do hypnotherapy for her, even if it was just to reduce the pain. But she wouldn't allow it.

It wasn't until two days later, when my youngest brother was enlisted into National Service, and my mum and I were in Pulau Tekong having a bus tour of the place.

In the bus, I told my mum, "I can see you're in pain. We've 5-10 minutes before we get off the bus. I can use this time to reduce your pain and potentially heal your arm. Would you allow me to do hypnotherapy with you?"

She finally agreed and I did a couple of modified techniques quickly.

By lunchtime in Pulau Tekong a couple of hours later, my mum's arm was back to normal and it had healed rather nicely, with only a bit of ache left in the wrist. My youngest brother saw it and exclaimed, "If you done it earlier, you wouldn't have to go through 2 days of pain and suffering!"

This incident started me thinking about how I can use my skills to help other people around me. Why do people choose to suffer in silence? Is it because they do not know of any solution? What if I start my own practice? What if I help others just like my mum, who decided to silently suffer instead of getting help? It wasn't long before I started my own hypnotherapy practice.

So by now, you've probably read about my analytical skills, my adaptability and not just quick but deep thinking too, which I attribute to my introversion!

In fact, I am very thankful to my friend for teaching me Chinese Chess. You probably already know that Chess involves some deep thinking and analysis, but did you know there is a variation of the game called Speed Chess? I didn't really mention because that will go into another story, but playing Speed Chess vastly improved the speed of my thoughts and processes.

Now I use these traits and skills to help my clients by adapting specific techniques to suit individual unique issues. Not to mention how natural it is for me to just listen to my clients, because being an introvert usually means we listen more than we speak! Once we start picking up certain cues, we can target the problem and use the right technique to get the clients the outcomes they are looking for.

To end my story, whether it is by chance, or whether it is meant to be, finding and growing a hidden talent can really be the factor to achieving success in life. Sometimes, all it takes is to realize what intrinsic traits you already have that's enough to develop into a full-fledged talent!

METAMORPHOSIS
ASHLEY ELLA CHOO

"Wow! Such a cheery baby. Can I carry her a while?"

That question never failed to pop up whenever my mum brought me out. I was a small bundle of joy. With sparkles in my eyes, I captured everyone's heart at first sight.

Born the eldest child in my family, I was a baby princess that had a heart-warming smile plastered on her face. I was adored by all the family members, receiving the entire portion of love and attention from my parents. I was a natural joy, embracing and enjoying every single moment of the limelight that was shone on me.

During those early years, I was vivacious and exuberant.

"Mummy! Mummy! I want to go to school, like the other kids!" I exclaimed and pointed excitedly to the group of children in their school uniforms playing at the playground.

"But you're only 3 years old. Too young," Mum responded with a tinge of annoyance. She was more pre-occupied with her task of lugging the heavy bags of groceries.

"But I want, can I? I promise to be a good girl and do my homework every day. Please…?"

After half a year of pestering and pleading, I was finally enrolled into kindergarten. I was only 4 years old. I enjoyed being with other children, playing games and learning new things. I enjoyed so much that I was even reluctant to go home when school was over. "RRRinggg!!!"

The school bell would ring incessantly. An entire group of children would stampede out from the classes. I just sat there staring at them. I was unable to comprehend their excitement at leaving school.

"Ashley, shall we leave now?" the gentle voice of my teacher, Mrs Tan, echoed in the empty classroom as I remained glued to my seat refusing to leave, "Your dad is waiting for you. I'm going to lock up already."

In such a way, two years of kindergarten soon flew by. I was a bright student and scored good grades.

"Well done Ashley! You top the class again!" Mrs Tan beamed at me, "I would like you to represent all the children and give a thanksgiving speech during the graduation ceremony. Oh! And also present a bouquet to Mrs Wong."

It would be my first time being on stage as well as giving a speech. Inside me was a starburst of euphoria that filled me with warmth and pride. On Graduation Day, I wore my prettiest dress. Mrs Tan applied some rouge and lipstick for me. My hair was braided with flowers and ribbons. My parents rushed to the front of the stage and the cameras clicked away.

Those were my early formative years, when I was adored, inquisitive and thirsty for adventure. I looked forward to primary school, the new things I would learn, books I would read. I would make new friends and we would play together. It was all going to be wonderful.

Unfortunately, my parents' plans did not seem to be in the same path.

"Ashley, Primary One already. Have to cut your hair," my mum instructed. She explained, "I don't have the time to plait for you every day."

Not only did she insist that I have my hair cut, she forced me to get it permed as well.

"No!" I wailed. I threw a tantrum, kicked up a big fuss. But it was of no use. Despite all my protests, my mum did not hear my pleas.

Being a young child, I was in no position to insist on having my way. I had to do as I was told. I followed her sullenly as she brought me to the salon and gave instructions to the hairdresser.

"Short! Short!"

I bit my lip as the scissors went 'snip snip'. When I saw my beautiful hair drop to the floor, tears started to roll down my cheeks.

It was a disaster to my long silky hair. The part of me that was thrilled to go to school was gone as with my long and beautiful hair. The exuberant side of me slowly died.

I started to keep to myself, hiding a sorrow within. This continued throughout my primary education. Instead of making many new friends, I kept with me only two very close friendships.

"Ashley! Want to take the bus with us after school?" my little friends would invite.

"No, I can't. My dad's coming to pick me up," I would reply monotonously.

Deep down, that wasn't me. I just allowed myself to fit into the mould that my parents carved for me.

During my adolescent years, I became more defiant and I wanted to express myself more.

Since young, I had always wanted my own study table, a bed of my own. I wished to have a room where I could hide and isolate myself from the world.

But I was the eldest of 5 siblings. To allow more comfort for my younger siblings who slept in the bedroom, I slept in the living room. We were a family of late sleepers, watching TV late into the night. I could not go to bed until the TV was off and everyone retired to their rooms. When the lights were out, I gritted my teeth in the darkness and cried myself to sleep every night. I yearned so badly for my personal space. I needed privacy.

Not getting enough solitude caused tension in my relationships with my parents and siblings. I was irritable and developed a foul temper. Resentment and anger, these were my bread and butter during my teenage years. I resented it. I could not understand it. Neither did my family.

"What's wrong with you?"

"Why can't you accompany and play with your brothers and sisters?"

"You're so selfish!"

Selfish.

This term was hot stamped in my heart at a tender age of 14. To avoid the continuous labelling, I knew I had to go under the radar by burying emotions and giving up my rights to voice my opinion. It was the only solution I had. There was no point talking. Everything was 'No'. Always negative.

"Can I go to McDonald's?"

"No!"

"Can I go to the movies?"

"No!"

"Can I go to my friend's birthday barbecue party?"

"No! You've to set a good example for your brothers and sisters. I don't want them to think that when they grow older they can do the same. What if they get led astray? Are you going to be responsible for it?" That was the type of reply I got every single time I asked. My heart shattered when my mum disallowed me to attend the party.

Soon, my friends stopped inviting me altogether. I cooped myself up at home, being the 'obedient' daughter my parents wanted me to be.

With the responsibility of being the good example upon my shoulders, my parents were very strict with me. I soon became the paradigm of a perfect child, obedient and disciplined. I was raised to care what people thought of me. I knew instinctively that my actions and behaviours were not solely my own. They represented my entire family.

It dawned on me that I had to live within the boundaries set by my parents and conform to the standards set by society. I then realized that I was not in the pilot seat of my life. I had lost my voice in life. I became nothing but an empty shell fulfilling my parents' wishes. I isolated myself.

Deep inside, a hatred starting building up. I hated who I was and whatever I was doing. I wanted to break free from these shackles that were holding me back. As a teenager, I did not know what to do, I was desolated and depressed. Inch by inch, I dug deeper the grave in my heart, throwing all thoughts and emotions into it.

During then, I did not know about introversion. I was not aware that I needed quiet spaces and time of solitude to recalibrate. I wish that I had known then. Perhaps, my life would have taken a different route. Perhaps, I would have found happiness sooner. Instead, the one thought that started seeding, was to grow up fast and get away from this congestion that was suffocating me. That was the only thought recurring in my mind, to leave my safe harbour, to leave the place many call home.

Time was like a brutal, cold-blooded killer. Ripping my teenage years straight out from my hands as I resisted it. But no one wins Time, no one was fast enough to hold on to it for 'Time waits for no man'. Soon, I was no longer a teen.

Growing up, I never got the recognition I needed to aid my confidence and self-esteem. It would become an issue that revolved around me even after setting foot in the workforce. I was afraid of rejection, thus I was never one initiating conversations and I absolutely loathed the thought of interaction with others.

For example, in the office pantry, my colleague Jill might casually ask as she poured herself a cup of coffee, "Are you coming to the party tonight?"

"No. Thanks," I would shut her off before she could continue, "I've a nice quiet evening planned with my take-out, a movie and a bottle of wine."

"Oh! Okay. But remember, you got to loosen up and have fun sometimes."

I would nod my head and scurry back to my work desk, shrugging off the conversation that had just happened.

Most of my colleagues had the impression that I was a boring and dull person, often cooped up at home and refusing to interact with the outside world. Some even had the misconception that I was being snobbish and aloof. Truth is, I appreciated the daily greetings and concern, but small talk was the bane of my existence.

I avoided the spotlight like vampires avoid sunlight. I shunned away from any attention and most definitely did not try to impress anyone at all. I hated to be the focal point of the crowd, preferring to blend in as that made me feel comfortable. I just wanted to relax and enjoy the company that I had. Just be present, without having to participate.

"Ashley, what song would you like to sing?" a question often shot at me at any karaoke session.

My typical answer would be a bashful smile, followed by a shake of the head. I was happy to sing along without having the microphone and I would be anyone's best cheerleader. But don't ask me to sing solo.

Beyond that facade I put up, I never failed to question if there was something amiss with myself. I hated myself for seeming so unfriendly and 'anti-social'. I always had this fantasy where I was all alone on a deserted island, taking a mini hiatus from work. Just me and my thoughts, ruminating on our nature of existence, and just about everything else that I wanted.

Then there was the constant battle of thoughts on whether I was born with this misanthropic personality. Or did I just grow up unable to tolerate being outgoing? I believed it had something to do with the environment I was brought up in. Most nights I pondered over the thought that if I had embraced the situations in my life with an open mind, I would probably have an entirely different personality right now. But usually, the thought went away as fast as it came.

When I got married, I felt so blissful. Finally, my dream of having a home of my own was fulfilled, happily doing up the little space for two.

A year later, I found my dream job - a full time mummy!

No boss, no colleagues, no meetings, no socializing. Life was a breeze at that point of time, though I was not entitled to annual leaves and had to work every day all year round. But I still had promotions, from being mother of one to mother of three!

My time to recharge was when all my little bosses went to bed and I had my alone time. I would do my favourite cross stitching and fix up jigsaw puzzles. I also found pleasure in stencil drawing on the kitchen cabinet, refrigerator, and bath room tiles. I simply enjoyed activities which involved just myself and the medium I was working with. During those times, my mind was truly calm and collected, feeling the peace within.

Unfortunately, my happiness was short-lived. After fifteen years of marriage, my husband and I parted ways. My family and friends were shocked.

"Huh? You're getting a divorce? What happened? Why?"

"Can't you endure for the sake of your children?"

"You're so selfish!"

Selfish! The label that I once buried within the depths of my mind surfaced yet again. All the excruciating pain of my teenage years came back. Was I really such a selfish person? I believed what other people thought of me as I could not hear my own voice that struggled to be heard.

My world crashed and collapsed when I lost custody of my three children. At that point of time, all I cried out for was words of solace from my mother to alleviate the emotional suffering that I was going through. But I received none of those. Instead, words of revilement cut straight through my heart.

Nothing hurts more than being unable to establish an emotional connection with one's own mother when at the rock-bottom of one's life.

My marriage was a hypnotizing experience for me. I realized that it was my form of escapism from my resentment and angst when growing up. Closing a chapter of fifteen years in my life was nothing short of grief and anguish.

After my divorce, I was convinced that my true self was fundamentally flawed. I buried her deep in the abyss of my heart.

"Life is just watching the hands on the clock move and knowing that time is slipping away by the second but not being able to do anything to reverse the fact and to accept it."

"Life is lost as with every breath we exhale."

For my children, I had to grit my teeth and fight on.

Over time, I adopted the life of a 'zombie'. I learnt to be alone. I no longer needed friends. I lost the passion to talk to people. The solitude I sought became an unhealthy reality; I easily put myself in quarantine for a long time. Being a thinker, I spent much time analysing, and it led to depression.

Gradually, my health deteriorated. I drowned myself with work and kept myself occupied. It was the only remedy to the excruciating pain I felt whenever the thought of losing my beloved children popped into my mind.

My condition was never let known to anyone for the fear of losing the access I had to see my children. Day in, day out, I put up a tough front, not letting anyone or anything get in touch with the vulnerable side of me. I fended off any words of care and concern, always with a smile, to hide my pain.

One morning, I woke up and found the ceiling of my room spinning non-stop. I blinked a couple of times and nothing changed. I slowly steadied myself up from bed and figured it was probably due to anaemia or hypoglycaemia. The truth struck me like a whirlwind when I found out I was suffering from Vertigo.

Dejected and worn out, I withdrew myself from the world further. Hiding in my shell that was my safe haven, I refused to step out for I did not want to face what had been planned for me. But, like a flower sprouting out from the rubble of an earthquake aftermath, my resilience gave me the courage that I desperately needed to surface from the hardship and blossom in the spring of life.

Breaking out from my cosy cocoon to take on life is one of my greatest goals. Fear and anxiety will follow. But, life is a peregrination of challenges. I can only choose to embrace it and brave on.

"Through joy and despair, through good health and sickness, life goes on regardless."

It is only now, a decade after the marriage broke up, that I am beginning the process of excavating my true self. I want back some of what I buried. I want the passion, the creativity, the wildness. I want the ultimate feeling of freedom that comes from being one's self regardless of whether or not others approve. I want these things together with the benefit of life's experience minus the teenage drama.

I started serving in a ministry in church to get my life back on track. Praising God, a live-and-let-live attitude naturally grew in me.

In 2013, I attended a spiritual retreat.

"Christ in us our cornerstone, we will go forth in Grace alone."

It was through this journey of faith that I dared to unveil myself again.

I realize now. I am introvert.

Many of my problems and heartaches stemmed from the fact that I was unaware of introversion and what it meant. I had struggled so much to fit into a mould that others expected and when I could not fit, I thought that something was very wrong with me. I had been miserable trying to conform. It left me tired and drained. I had hated myself without knowing why.

If only I had known back then, as I do now, I would have been saved from so many years of anguish.

Introversion is my nature; it is not a problem about me. For too long, I had always viewed it as a flaw. But in fact, it is neither a defect nor an illness. It is simply the way I dispense my energy and re-charge, that's all. Yes, I am different, but there is nothing wrong with being different. In a world that makes too much noise, as an introvert, I only need some quiet time to myself.

Accepting introversion as my nature, I look at life from a whole new point of view. I become aware that understanding myself and my place in this world is a key aspect to the success of my life. This is the moment I truly found the real me.

I finally comprehend what I could not for years, that when I accept who I am, I attract like-minded people and the right set of circumstances. This is more important than trying to win the approval of people who will never understand or appreciate the real me.

I am more confident socially and meeting new people has become a breeze for me. I have re-discovered my generous spirit. Given my personality, I am never one who works for reward, but often for the pure satisfaction of my heart and the sense of accomplishment. I give without the expectation of receiving in return. I am at peace with myself, happy in the knowledge finally, that I am not a selfish person as others had mistakenly labelled me.

Often people come up to me asking, "Why are you so quiet?"

Little do they know that I possess the confounding ability to rattle on about my life, my goals and my dreams for hours! However, I only open up to the small group of people who hold a special place in my vulnerable heart. My sharp witty humour reveals itself when I am with friends I trust. A quiet spirit doesn't mean boring by any means.

Neither am I shy nor anti-social, I enjoy going out with friends and have strong social skills. I merely need some downtime after socializing to recharge my soul.

I cherish friendship very much. Being a great listener and also sensitive enough to be conscious of the contents of your heart, that's my forte. This level of intimacy and vulnerability cannot afford to be wounded or disturbed.

It definitely takes a plethora of trust and understanding before I am able to bring down my barriers before someone. I will be the best friend that anyone can have, defending them and remaining by their side even when the odds are against them. But a paucity of distrust is enough for me to bring the barriers back up, and the friendship would be nothing more than a memory.

Now that I recognize and acknowledge my introversion, I understand myself better. I know my values and what I want to get out of life. By embracing my introvert traits, I live the life of my own design, not by other people's definitions. I do things that I most enjoy. Cross-stitching, jigsaw puzzles, stencil drawing. When I immerse totally in it, I am calm and energised. My universe is centred. And I produce very good work.

This self-awareness makes me more confident, attractive, and sophisticated. But of course, behind all of that is a woman who still feels most safe in her cocoon, solitary confinement. I just typically do not showcase awesomeness for everyone to see.

It is painful for me to open up and talk about my past. But I want to share my story. If there is someone who reads my story, who went through the same turbulence, I want to encourage them to accept their uniqueness. Introversion is not abnormal, not anti-social, not selfish. It's just the way one is.

In fact, telling my story now is even more cathartic for me. I reconcile with myself and my family. No need for apologies or forgiveness from either side, since nobody was wrong or right. For even I did not know what it was all about, so how could anyone else? They may still not comprehend, but it's alright because now at least I understand myself.

As I shed the burden of my history, my heart is lighter. My soul is free. I am finally comfortable in my own skin, and with that comes new confidence and courage. One right step and everything else falls into place. I am no longer a misfit.

Today, as I bring light to my story, I am a new me. Confident and spirited! And I do the most unselfish thing now, by sharing my pain and most importantly, the path of my healing.

I grew from the innocence of a child into a desolated teen. What I did not know was that during my time in my chrysalis, when I felt trapped in a world so dark, I was growing and preparing myself to emerge as a strong and beautiful woman, like a butterfly.

In summary, introverts are amazing people with rich hidden depths, and if you are one, rejoice! Claim your place in this noisy world that talks too much. Spread your wings and fly.

THE BUTTERFLY - Living Introversion Flaunting Elegance (L.I.F.E)

Living Introversion Flaunting Elegance

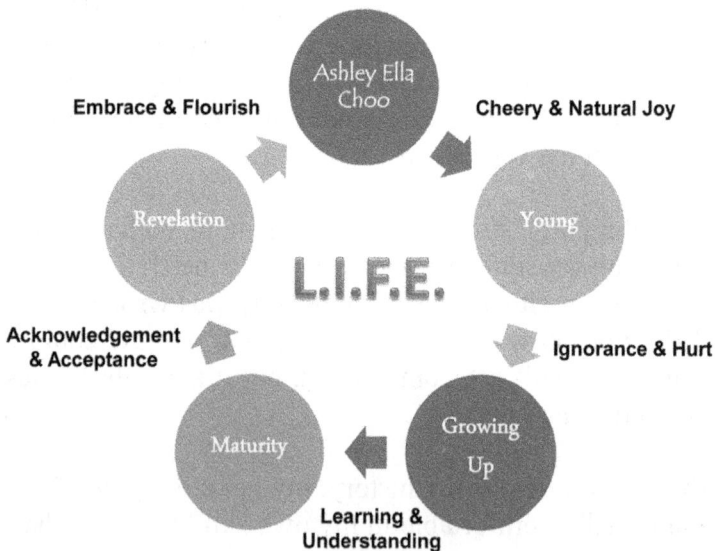

Embrace & Flourish

Ashley Ella Choo

Cheery & Natural Joy

Revelation

Young

L.I.F.E.

Acknowledgement & Acceptance

Ignorance & Hurt

Maturity

Growing Up

Learning & Understanding

CREATIVE EXPRESSION -
THE LIFEBLOOD OF AN INTROVERT
HAZRIQ IDRUS

I bumped into an old school friend the other day. We were from the same class in Primary School. What she said to me was really surprising...

"You're not the Hazriq I remember. So different now! You were so quiet back then! Now I see you act on stage and television. Give talks. Everyone's surprised. We can't believe. What had happened?"

She was right. I was a very quiet student. In fact, I was so quiet that I didn't even dare to raise my hands to answer questions from my teachers. When I won awards that required me to collect on stage, I trembled. I was very quiet and shy.

It got me thinking, "Did something actually happen? What happened?"

I remember vividly a performance back in my secondary school days. Every class had to take part in a National Day performance competition event and I was one of those being 'volunteered' to represent my class, together with a few others. During the performance, at one point, I had to step forward and rally the audience to sing a chorus of the National Day song together with us on stage.

I rallied, "Come on! Come on! Join us sing!"

What happened next?

The whole school kept quiet! Not a single soul joined me and my team to sing the chorus. To add more salt to the wound, the very next day my other schoolmates kept teasing me, "Come on! Come on!" That was one of the most embarrassing moments in my life. Worst of all, we did not win the competition. I felt that I had let myself and the team down. I needed to go somewhere – an avenue - to express my disappointments!

However as I reflected those days, it dawned on me that the experience actually pushed my 'disappointments' to another level. As introverts, we are healers of emotional wounds. I overcame that moment of disappointment by starting a 'project' to find out how stage performers managed to exude that confidence on stage to capture and influence the audience.

This search brought me to theatre. After watching a short theatre play by the actors while I was in junior college, I sensed that there is so much to learn doing acting and theatre works. I was interested to know more.

My acting and theatre journey started in 1997. After that 'big break', passing an audition for a major theatre production that was to be held at Victoria Theatre, I embarked on my first steps learning about acting and theatre.

During the practice and rehearsal sessions, I found a new platform - a platform to express my ideas and my feelings.

Introverts are good at studying. The love and passion for learning helps me to seek continuous improvements for personal and professional growth. I learnt the ropes from various theatre practitioners to hone my acting skills. I enjoy watching and learning the acting and theatre skills, to apply during my own performances.

Vocal techniques, stage presence, stage dynamics are some of the skills I picked up from my mentors.

In fact, one of the first few acting skills I learnt was 'theatre improvisation'. Theatre improvisation helps us actors to be able to think and react on the spot. This is crucial because stage acting is 'Live' performance; and if anything goes wrong, as actors we must be able to 'ad-lib' and continue with the show – as if nothing had gone wrong - for the audience. (Ad-lib is a term in theatre; originally from the Latin word 'Ad-Libtum', which means to improvise, impromptu or delivery without preparation).

This is the one thing about being an introvert. If we are passionate about something, we are really passionate about it. I was so passionate (and I still am now!) about acting, little did I realize that the skills in acting and theatre had helped me in other aspects of my life.

In the year 2002, I was balancing theatre works and working with one of the government agencies. I was a newbie at the agency back then. As a newbie, I had to host a corporate event, emceeing in front of corporate executives, staff and vendors. There were about 1,000 people in the audience.

At the event that I was to emcee, I had to play 'James Bond' who was looking out for his 'Bond Girl' (who would be my co-host for the event) in the audience. So the event organizer played a pre-enacted video clip of me (as James Bond; but ala 'Get Smart' character) speaking but using my shoe as a phone.

After the video clip had been played, I had to 'continue' with the storyline by appearing on stage. That was the nerve-wrecking moment, for sure! And to make matters worse, just as I was about to speak and address the audience, the microphone died on me! How much worse could it get?

Luckily, my theatre and acting experiences took over, and that helped me - a LOT – in managing my nerves. The improvisation skills helped me deal with the fiasco of the event - the faulty microphone!

What did I do?

Almost instantaneously, I 'replaced' the microphone with my shoe (similar to the one in the video clip). I had the audience in stitches because they could relate it to the video clip earlier. This was done to 'buy time' while the organizer looked for a replacement microphone.

I did not realize it then, but the opportunity to speak to that particular group of people at the corporate event helped me greatly in my professional capacity.

One of the ways an introvert can grow is by experimenting and having new experiences. Through that experience, I started to get more hosting gigs in the company, the other staff and directors started taking notice of me, and all these helped me in climbing up the corporate ladder!

By applying the theatre improvisation skills I had learnt, it helped me as an actor to respond well when things go in a different direction on stage. Off stage, I feel empowered because I know I am self-sufficient. I can apply the theatre improvisation skills to manage any curve ball that life might throw at me.

I stayed with the company until I received my Long Service Award of 10 years, before parting ways amicably to start my own business consultancy and start writing books. In fact, my former director lent his support by writing his testimonial of me which I gladly placed it at the cover page of my first book, 'The Stage Fright Antidote!'

People keep asking me how, after doing acting and speaking for some years, I can appear confident on stage all the time and yet I am still an introvert.

To me, there are two aspects to acting that I figured out.

Firstly, acting on stage is about taking up different characters and immersing in the feelings of the characters. Introverts are very in touch with our own feelings. We can relate to the feelings of people we know, or even the feelings of the human life in general. This is what 'being in other people's shoes' really means.

I found acting to be a natural way to express oneself. True enough, as an actor, our feelings are one of our greatest assets. We are trained to control feelings and emotions to exude them on stage when necessary. Off stage, we are able to use this important skill to empathize with others and be a good listener for others.

Secondly, it is the art of playing different roles at different situations. We could be a father back home to our kids, a big brother to our younger siblings, or even a buddy back in army camp during reservist, but ultimately we are the exact same person. It is the roles we play at different settings that define us differently. It is an added advantage to the introvert because introverts like to connect with the essence of life.

When I first started to act, my main intention was not about becoming famous or being a celebrity. As an introvert, that sounded intimidating to me; in fact, I thought it was a daunting task to be doing.

I just wanted an outlet to perform, to express my ideas and spread my messages. As I reflect my life journey, thinking through about my 'transformation', I found that as humans, especially introverts, we need a platform to express ourselves.

Creative expression is the lifeblood of the introvert. It could be in the form of painting, sculpturing or any form of arts. For me, I found my passion in acting.

So, to answer my primary school classmate's question on "What happened?", actually, nothing has happened. I am still what I was before.

Recently a friend asked me to take an online introvert quiz. The result is the same - I am an introvert. The only difference is that I now understand more about being an introvert and I'll find opportunities to maximize the skills that introverts have, to make a difference in others.

Beyond acting for stage or television, I started my business consulting company for this one single mission – which is to spread the message that theatre and acting techniques are useful life-skills. It is also important to note that one does not need to be an actor to learn those skills because they are universal and when applied, can accelerate one's confidence for personal and professional growth.

FROM RABBITS TO EAGLES
JUDY KOH

Born in 1963, in the year of the rabbit according to the Chinese zodiac sign, I exhibited traits of a stereotypical, introverted rabbit - quiet, shy, preferring to stay in my own burrow. Since young, I was a serious, intense kid who kept to myself and did not smile readily. Reading, painting, music and poetry were activities which I thoroughly enjoyed on my own.

In school, all the way to the university, I was a serious, focused student who had strong, intense views about topics concerning the world. Sometimes it would seem as if the weight of the world's problems was on my shoulders and writing poems was an outlet to air my intense feelings. Neither did I enjoy big parties nor idle chatter. Being in a crowd, surrounded by loud and garrulous people was a stressful thing for me. I was not impolite or unfriendly; I just did not enjoy mixing with people whom I did not know, preferring quiet solitude. Neither was I a wall flower nor the life of the party. Staying in a quiet corner, observing the rest of the people was something I was more comfortable with.

Since I excelled in school and was regarded to be a dependable and responsible student, teachers and classmates often selected me to take on leadership roles. I was a class monitor, leader and a head prefect in my school. However, though I accepted the roles knowing that it was an honour to be given such responsibilities, I was a reluctant leader and did not particularly enjoy it. As a leader, I often had to give speeches in school. This was not as stressful as when I was surrounded by crowds after the speech when I had to engage in polite talk with them.

Later on, when I became an entrepreneur in my 40s, and started Caffe Pralet, a bakery cum restaurant and a culinary and bakery school, Creative Culinaire The School, "networking" was an activity highly recommended to me by my entrepreneur friends. However, networking sessions were not sessions that I was fully comfortable with. Perhaps I regarded it as a 'necessary evil" since I desired to grow my business, forge new relationships and needed to tell the world about my business. Hence, I coerced myself to attend networking events and viewed it as part of my responsibility as a boss of the two companies I was running. But I could not shake off the feeling that networking seemed at times disingenuous when I had to engage in small and polite talk. More often than not, I found myself wanting to leave early.

There were other challenges too in running the business as an introverted leader. Most of the time, I felt inadequate and not fully equipped as a leader. Leaders who are extroverts would be able to rally their team with words, exuberance and enthusiastic, positive energy. They are usually more generous in their verbal encouragement and praise. But I had difficulties in all these areas.

There were also well meaning customers who advised me that as a boss, I needed to be more 'diva-like", more outgoing, approachable and friendlier with people who came to my café and school. Their advice was that I needed to "work the crowd", as they put it, as that would help me to build more support for my business. Many times I tried to do that, only to find myself running quickly back to the kitchen to hide, unhappy and uncomfortable. Even when I willed myself to appear in the café, I actually found myself wishing that customers would not recognize me as "Chef Judy"! A sense of defeat, discouragement would sometimes creep into my heart and make me wonder if God had only made me a friendly, outgoing extrovert, I could perhaps then be a better businesswoman and a more successful boss.

Before long, I was struggling with strong, crippling feelings of inadequacy and inferiority complex.

One day, while reading the book of Moses in the Bible, it came as a surprise to me that Moses was also an introvert like me! God had called him to be a leader among the Israelites and to lead them through the wilderness. And like me, he was a reluctant leader. When Moses objected to God at the burning bush, saying that he was not an eloquent speaker and to send someone else instead, God assured Moses that He would be with him and teach him what to say.

Gradually, as I spent more time studying the Bible and grew in my Christian walk, I realized that me, born as an introvert, was not an accident. It says in the Bible, "I will praise You for I am fearfully and wonderfully made; Marvelous are Your works, And that my soul knows very well."

The realization that I was born an introvert with a God-given purpose made me not only appreciate my traits as an introvert but also taught me to harness my strengths as an introverted leader. My ability for example, to spend time alone to reflect on the purpose and mission of my work, envisioning and planning for the bigger picture kept me focused and determined in my journey, despite all the ups and downs along the way. Although I had strong and clear views myself, I was always conscious of the fact that every individual on my team was important and I would listen to their views, study them carefully for telltale signs that could indicate their true feelings towards their work and our company.

Although I stayed firm on setting standards expected from my staff, I was also sensitive about how they felt, even if I might have just given them a stern lecture if things were not going properly. Deep in my heart was also a genuine concern for my team's welfare and a determination to guide my staff to grow and build a better future together.

As an introverted businesswoman in the very competitive Food and Beverage business, the ability to reflect, think and dream about ways to achieve my mission together with my staff on board injected vitality and creativity to the business. I found myself looking for leaders and planning how to train them so that when the time was ripe, the baton could be passed to them to continue the race.

Furthermore, the realization that I was born an introvert with a purpose and that God would open doors for me in my business if He wanted to, took the pressure off me to "have to" network aggressively for my business in order to close deals. This led to a calm and relaxed attitude towards networking, business and life in general. In short, I was much happier and a lot less stressed. Learning to be more appreciative, positive and loving towards people around me was part of the transformation.

I began to reach out more to my staff and business associates in love and patience, instead of clamping up like an oyster and running away to avoid meeting people who were "not my kind". Through the years, I believe God has brought people who are different from me, people who are extroverts for example, to complement and work with me on various successful projects.

Indeed, today, I embrace and appreciate the fact that I am an introvert called to be a leader, destined for greater things in life. Instead of being a rabbit hiding in the burrow, I am now the eagle with the vision to soar to greater heights with my staff and a clear mission to grow and prosper my business to be greater blessings to others. No longer do I feel inadequate in my abilities or do I envy extroverts. I guess such is the transformative power of God.

Indeed, I am "fearfully and wonderfully made".

OYSTERS

Like oysters we keep our shells closed.

Sometimes, peep just a little to let the world in...

a grain of sand perhaps, some strange splinter enters,

irritates and our shells struggle to close

but layers of nacre coat and polish the pearl within us

takes time, but we don't give up

till the pearl is formed and then we shine

in God's glory and our shells open

for all the world to see.

[signature]
25/2/16

CLIMB EVERY MOUNTAIN
FIONA TAN-LOW

Never offer an introvert 'a penny for your thoughts', unless you're prepared to go bankrupt.

Just so you know where your money goes, let me describe what it's like inside my head when I think.

First, there is the decision tree, a magnificent rain tree with a glorious canopy. Every situation has many possible actions, with many ways of getting done. If this, then this. Each idea branching out, out, out. I've hundreds, maybe thousands of decision trees. There's a forest in my head!

Just like the mythical Sun Wukong, I also have lots of mini-me's, many little fionas, with ideas and opinions of their own they don't hesitate to share. They swing from the branches of my decision trees, chattering non-stop. They are my decision pickers. Also, my wet blankets and cheerleaders.

It's not weird. Not crazy. It's just the way I think, perhaps a little bit too much. Maybe that's why I appear quiet or slow. By the time I rummage through my forest, reach the correct tree and then scramble back out with what to say, peeling the wrong little fionas from off my legs, the conversation is already over.

But it is by choice.

Like the loris, I'm slow when I want, swift if I need. Oftentimes, I don't need.

I'm shy. I remember, as a child, buying sweets at the shop. All the kids would clamber at the display racks, tapping their ten cent coins on the plastic containers. I simply hung back and waited to be noticed. Until the uncle asked, "Xiao-mei-mei, what you want?"

This behavioural trait continued in adulthood, where I spent my entire working career in office administration. Cocooned in back-end offices, I was happiest in my own small cubicle, all the people I dealt with safely behind computer screen. If I didn't meet a single soul throughout the day, BEST!

In the Representative Offices of MNCs where I worked, I got to know many colleagues and clients, mostly based overseas. They, including their spouses and families, are now my lifelong friends even though we have never met and probably never will.

I did good work and wished to be promoted, but I never clambered for it. Nobody knew; I never spoke up. I simply waited to be noticed.

"Fiona, go lah! Talk to the big boss lah. Saka a bit! Don't hide in your corner," people encouraged me.

I would shake my head and retreat even further.

"Why not? Scared what?"

"I hate making small talk," was all I could mumble in reply, "especially with big shots."

What.

"How was your flight? Which hotel are you staying in? Yes, it's very hot this time of year. Oh, you want to try durian? Yes, yes, smells like sewer. Haha. Yes, just like your blue cheese, yes. Hahaha."

Superficial meaningless nothings! Big Boss didn't travel halfway around the globe to discuss with me the difference between D24 and Mao Shang Wang! I'm sure he didn't care for durian at all, in the same way I didn't care for blue cheese.

I also assisted with Marketing duties, usually after-sales support and customer service. Short of going out to meet clients, I could handle almost everything else. Do you know that character 'Wang YuYan' from Louis Cha's 'Tian Long Ba Bu'? Yes that's me, knowing all the gungfu steps but never actually going out to fight.

Via email, I could mediate and resolve many disputes. A colleague once said I could 'talk the bird down from the tree'. But face-to-face? One big blubbery mess! When it was over, my trembling subsided and my breathing back to normal, I would re-enact the scene in my head, substituting each jibberish I had blurted with a different rebuttal. For days, weeks, months. Then, one fine day, maybe in the MRT or somewhere, I would go, "Yes! I should've said that!"

Quiet, slow, unnoticeable. Can't handle a decent quarrel to save my life. I don't suppose those were quite the qualities for entrepreneurship. So when I started my own business, I surprised many people, including myself.

It wasn't some mundane backend work-from-home business like bookkeeping or data entry. No. I was going to get out there and change the way the spa industry operated. For 33,000 people! Victims of spa closures, who suffered from contract packages with unused balances they could no longer redeem. I was going to champion the cause, fight for their rights. I would galvanize them. Stand up! Speak out! Down with hardsell tactics! Out with contract packages! I would go up against big spa operators and pressure them to run their businesses more responsibly. Beat the chest and punch the air! RA-RA-RA!

Oh dear.

I remember, the first time I stepped into a spa was merely to enquire the price for getting a facial. Four hours of ginger tea later, when I emerged from the manager's room, the shopping mall was already in darkness. The drowsy hum from the cleaners' vacuuming machines added to my dazed state of mind. The security guard yawned as he let me out through a side door into the back alley. I didn't get any facial done that night but I had become $10,000 poorer, with 4 credit cards maxed out.

"What happened to you? What were you thinking? Sign so many packages you don't even know for what?" my husband chided me, incredulous.

"I don't know! Honestly, I don't know!" in cold sweat with buyer's remorse, I wrung my hands.

Now, looking back, I know. I just couldn't say "No!". I did not want to reject people; they might miss their sales quota and lose their commission. I could not hurt their feelings. I was too kind. I cared too much.

So, by virtue of my $10,000 spa package, I enjoyed a whole spectrum of spa treatments. Tranquil. Detox. Go in naked. Come out recharged. I had found my Shangri-La!

However, I also witnessed the unpleasant goings-on. Hardsell, bad service, poor standards, spa closures. A pity, for an industry that was all about love and care. Something so beautiful, mired in such ugliness. Signs of trouble in paradise?

The second spa I signed with was a sanctuary even more beautiful. I won't go into the details because you might start drooling.

"No problem ah? Y'all won't suddenly pack up and close down ah?" pen poised above the dotted line, I was smart enough to ask.

"Aiyo, Fiona-ah! Look around. Does it look like we're in trouble?"

Hm, that's true. The place was abuzz with sales executives and rich customers. The raised parquet floor, with recessed coloured lighting, echoed with the footsteps of the well-heeled. Tok! Tok! Tok! Yes, that must be how success sounds like. All my little fionas, seduced and intoxicated with the good life in spa paradise, weren't too lucid when they agreed the signs were assurance enough.

One month later, this second spa was transferred to yet another, supposedly as a form of strategic takeover. I felt like an unwanted child fostered away to a stepmother.

"No problem ah? Y'all not closing down ah?"

"Aiyo, Miss Fiona! Where can have problem? They want to focus on other core business, and we want to expand. Baru just take over, where can have problem?"

The damned place tanked within three months.

At the time this 'foster-stepmother' spa shut down, I was at home, nursing a broken foot. While people went to Small Claims Tribunal and creditors' meetings, I hobbled at home, not any less angry at being unable to redeem $3,800 worth of unused packages. Oh, Hell hath no fury like a woman with a broken foot, sweet-talked and hard-sold by two spas consecutively, with no good service in return, and money still in their bank!

And that was how Blue Moon Valley was born.

It was a shit idea.

Not because it's lousy, but because I created it while doing a number two. Toilet inspiration? I've buckets of it! I don't represent all introverts when I say this but really, my best thinking is done in the toilet. With the mirror my conscience, I am most true unto myself. Purging of toxins clears my mind so. Brilliant sparks of ideas shoot and whizz by, haloed by intentions that glow pure, noble and sincere.

As they say, "Some go there to read and wonder, some go there to think and ponder". So there I was in my throne room, pondering. My idle mind mused over the sorry state of the spa industry.

"So, what do we have here?" I did what introverts do best, analyse the situation to death.

Spas - closed

Owners - nowhere to be found

Members - upset, no satisfactory way to redeem their unused packages

Lawyers say, "Caveat Emptor."

Banks say, "Pay up!"

So, what was I left with? What were 33,000 of us left with? This was a wrong that must be righted! Someone must come out and make things better. Someone had to make a difference. Bring back the love. I therefore decided. If no-one was going to do it, I would.

Poised on the most powerful seat, I, the spa queen, rode through my forest of decision trees, like Lady Godiva in Coventry. I gathered my army of little fionas and, with my 30 years administrative management background, I designed an entire fool-proof system. One that would bring respectability back to the industry, return power to consumers and ensure that spas perform and give good quality. It was actually a workable business model!

I decided to do this business and named it Blue Moon Valley.

"So, how? What do you think?" I sought opinion.

"Wow! It's great!" everybody was impressed.

"Go for it, Fion!"

So I did. I forgot one very important thing. The mountains before the valley.

The first mountain, apparently, was also seated on the throne looking back at me from the mirror.

"Sure or not? You can meh?"

And then, it hit me with a whammy, "You're an introvert!" As if there ought to be things that introverts couldn't do?

I looked up this sheer wall of absolute granite, a foreboding mountain of self-doubt and unnecessary self-deprecation that had prevented me from doing so many things I knew I could. For the first time in my life, I realized that through introversion, I had been blessed with an incredible efficient forest of decision trees, and little fionas who check and double-check my every move. But I had allowed both to go rampant. Instead of controlling them, I had let them control me.

Well, not anymore!

I took charge, weeded the ground, trimmed the branches, scrubbed and disciplined the little fionas. When everybody else had confidence in me, I was a fool to doubt myself. My little fionas chipped away at self-doubt, and cleared the debris where immediately, confidence flooded in.

By nature, myriad of thoughts go randomly in my head, of no value maybe even damaging, if left untended. But just like the elements of sun, wind and water, when I took charge and harnessed these thoughts, they were converted into energy and the power generated was tremendous.

Therefore, my introversion itself became the sturdy foundation on which I built the business. My base camp, so to speak.

Once I won over myself, there was no stopping me. I proceeded to draw up a business plan. Transferred my toilet paper doodles to more respectable A4 typewritten format.

Did I say there was no stopping me? Sorry! Spoke too soon! Even before I rounded the bend, the next mountain loomed ahead.

I'm a perfectionist. This is the reason why I don't put out as many things as I know I'm capable of. I'm simply never satisfied that it's already the best. What I consider as holding back in the name of perfectionism, others call it procrastination. So this mountain had twin peaks, boon and bane.

I realized that perfectionism and procrastination had been resident in my nature. Life is a cruise, it had never bothered me one way or the other. But, having taken on a social responsibility, I had to change gear. Wow! I maneuvered this mountain like an ice road trucker! Ease up on perfectionism here! Cut back on procrastination there! As what they say in Hokkien, 'Tak yew! Tak brake!'

Being perfectionist, I am my own worst critic. By the same token, I'm my own best supporter. Perfect is perfect. When it's ready, it's ready. Spaghetti, al dente, is perfect. And if I waited for the shallots and garlic to turn golden brown before turning off the flame, they would end up 'chao tar'. Following this Aglio Olio theory, I consciously avoided over-polishing.

I set deadlines and committed to them by announcing to people. Without a finishing line, the race for perfectionism would keep going round the tracks. My business plan for a unique and game-changing concept, was therefore completed on time. And since, as an introvert, I think of everything from all possible angles, I was also assured it was ready and perfect.

What had at first seemed an obstacle then was actually a golden mountain, and I owned it. I only needed to recognize gold in its raw form and acquire the techniques to mine it.

When it came time to bring to market, on my launch date 17 April 2011, I hit another mountain so terrifying, I dared not even look at it! Just being in its shadow made me wretchedly sick. So far, all the things I accomplished had been in the safety of my toilet or behind computer screen. Now, I was venturing further. At the launch, I would have to meet people, many of them strangers! And, horrors! I'd have to give a speech! The reality tumbled on me like boulders from the rockslide.

Fortunately, my little fionas visualized me a launch party, complete with welcome speech and many members signing up. For days, awake or asleep, I was at my party. The venue was awash in hues of blue and yellow, my corporate colors. The flowers I googled to learn which grew in valleys, adorned the tables, their petals tremulous in the breeze. The Pointer Sisters belted 'I'm So Excited! Ah-ha! Ah-ha!'. My steps were choreographed to the beat of the song as I ran in slapping palms and giving high fives. Woohoo!

Not everything happened as I imagined, but at least I scraped through, having lived it for days in my head.

To grow my membership fast exponentially, I took my concept to the big companies to secure corporate accounts. I would be their dedicated "Spa Concierge", in much the same way as they used to have a Travel Ticketing Agent (before the days of online bookings).

To many people, "spa" was, and still is, a dirty word. It was difficult getting through people's suspicion and skepticism, a thick flatulent fog left by the smelly reputation of a few bad spas. People had been so jaded, they suspected and pre-judged me even though I was there to help. They avoided me like the plague.

"Buzz off!" (Actually something harsher but only this was printable.)

"No thanks!" another common curt reply, "I kena before already. I don't want."

"I still have a few more sessions with my current contract, let me finish it first," a kinder sidestep.

This mountain was tough because, firstly, I had to meet strangers and, secondly, deal with their mistrust. But it was exactly those who shunned me that needed me most! So, I gave the best of all that I'm made of - sincerity, love, care. Being a good listener and very sensitive to people's feelings, I'm a natural for service industry. I'm not pretty, but I've a big bright smile. Not brainy, just funny. Possess no power except for a ton of compassion. Armed with all that is second nature to me, I broke the ice, melted anger and thawed suspicion.

"Let your Valley Godmother provide and protect you," I began.

"What d'you mean, the safer, smarter, savvier way to spa?" people would ask, disbelief and curiosity evident in their voices.

"Safer because as my member, there're many of you. Smarter because I use different methods that are better for you."

"Then, 'savvier' neh?"

"We conduct ourselves with class and grace."

"Don't understand."

"Just because we had felt bullied and manipulated by the spas, doesn't mean we've to bully them back. We're a vehicle for reconciliation, not revenge."

"OK, so how do you reconcile us?"
It was very gratifying to see my members' excitement and enthusiasm when they realized how they could have the power of choice and freedom back in their hands.

"That's so ingenuous!" one HR executive had exclaimed in awe. He turned to his colleagues, "How come we never think of this?"

"Can give me some more application forms? I'll ask my friends to sign too," was the next most heartening comment.

Concurrently, I negotiated with spa operators for services and discounts. Going up to the big players was daunting as hell. They were Goliaths, I wasn't even David. I was nobody. Their offices were so grand and imposing. One of them, I remember, was so gargantuan its water feature alone was bigger than my office!

Yet, I was going to ask these people to collaborate and work according to my terms, a 180 degree departure from their modus operandi. I had no idea how they would react. With no basis of reference, I imagined terrible things. The spa operators would laugh, they would scorn, shred me to pieces. Buzz me off. My little fionas shrank and went soft in the knee. The lousier ones fainted and fell off the decision trees, dropping like flies.

Stop! Pep talk! I only needed to see it as yet another challenge and not approach from angle of ignorance or fear. This mountain was new and unchartered territory. It had a K2 face! But all it needed was more thorough recce. Better preparation, better equipment, training, acclimatization. In introvert terms, this meant more thoughts, more analyses, and more mental rehearsals.

Like a mountaineer who checked his ropes and pulleys, I would leave my office fully prepared. At the spas, I'd pace the floor, rehearsing. When they were ready to see me, I'd go in, head up, shoulders back, chest out. Heart in my throat, throbbing so hard I felt like a frog.

The first question was usually more than a slap in the face.

"Sorry? Blue what? Blue Valley? Oh! Blue Moon Valley......
Never heard of it!"

"That's why I'm here to share with you."

"Why the name so funny one?"

"It's the place near Shangri-La where, in James Hilton's novel "Lost Horizon", everybody lived happily in peace and never grew old."

All questions fired at me from machine gun, whilst I struggled to re-load my puny little slingshot.

"What? No hardsell? Then how're we expected to get your members?"

"I'm their concierge. I buy for my members. I don't sell for you. If you're good, my members will come again. That's repeat business for you."

"But you don't allow us to sign contract packages with your members?"

"Your contract is with me. My members come to you under Blue Moon Valley account. This is the protection I give my members."

"And what's this Pay-Per-Use? Who pays?"

"My members pay me. I pay you."

"So difficult! We can't get the money upfront?"

"That's the biggest bugbear of my members, and the reason why they're not coming to you. Hence I do it differently. This is one segment you cannot get back. Through Blue Moon Valley, it may be possible."

"Very hard leh."

"Not really. Instead of having one customer X number of times, you now have X customers coming each time. 1 times 10, 10 times 1."

"How much discount must we give your members?"

"It's up to you. How attractive you want to be. The concept is for you to attract my members with the right pricing. And retain them with your good service."

"I just don't see how it benefits us to sign with you. How many members do you have?"

And that would be when all my mental target practices paid off. No more BRRrrrat-a-tat-tat!!! of machine-gun but Pop! Pop! Pop! from my trusted slingshot, as I elaborated the advantages of working with Blue Moon Valley.

"That's interesting!" the spas would come round, "I think it's very noble, what you're trying to do. I don't see that it will help me much. But I don't see any harm either. OK, we'll give it a try!"

For the record, I was often well received both by members and spas, especially after the initial barricades. For members to call it 'ingenuous' and spas to think it 'noble', was a very rewarding affirmation.

And then, something wonderful happened.

I had started out being member-centric, protecting members from undesirable tactics employed by spa operators. But, working with many vendors confirmed my early sentiments that although every spa was suspect, not every spa was guilty. They deserved a fair trial.

The idea of changing the industry ought not to effect such a reversal as to over-compensate members at the expense of the spas. Rather, both sides should be served equally and neither one should look upon the other as enemy. The real equilibrium is when both parties reconcile and harmony is restored. This was what I meant when I created my slogan - "the safer, smarter, savvier way to spa". I marvelled at my own great foresight to have thought so far ahead, that took me a while to catch up with myself.

Not only was I best placed to mend ties and bridge the chasm, I was also emotionally most invested and well equipped. I'm a good mediator, who would go on to forge lifelong friendships with members and vendors. My mission took on greater sense of purpose. My work became more meaningful and impactive.

The day will come when the spa industry is good again, no hardsell, prepaid packages. Even if there are spa closures, there will be no more spa-victims. I will look in the mirror and know. An introvert did it.

I went on to do many things which were normally averse to my introvert self. I took part in road shows and visited at BNI breakfast meetings. I even served on the executive committee of a women's club that I'd secretly admired since 1980's.

Sometimes I wonder. What propelled me to do the things I didn't ordinarily like, or dare, to do? I was neither hungry nor greedy for money, fame or power. What was it then that fuelled this fire in my belly? I realized that Blue Moon Valley is a vehicle driven by love, fuelled by passion, and introversion is the engine.

I cared enough, for something bigger and more powerful than myself, to step forward and serve. This need far outweighed any fears. Timid for myself I might be, but I was brave for others when needed.

Sure, the mountains will always be there. The climb will be tough. But I'm prepared, resilient and confident. At the top, I can see further. The other side is the same, nothing to be afraid of!

My forest of decision trees is now a cultivated plantation. The soil of imagination is fertile. Seeds of ideas yield bumper harvests of fruitful thoughts. All my little fionas are untapped resources with infinite potential, their combined charge a powerful force to be reckoned.

The loudness of the world and high energy of people may overwhelm me. But it does not mean any superiority in size, power, or intellect. People may laugh at me. People may judge. So what?

As Mr Lee Kuan Yew once said (in a different context), "They think they are superior, I don't think I'm inferior." That outlook resonates with me and as an introvert, I stand proud.

SUCCESS IS A CHOICE
VERN LAI

There are so many angles from which I can share in this chapter on how I triumph as an introvert. Perhaps talking about my childhood to how I am today? How about the mindset shift? Or perhaps my journey in business and how the challenges have helped me in my personal growth? Whichever the direction, you can tell that I think a lot. Sometimes, I analyze till I get paralyzed, mentally.

Before I fall into deep thought, let me give you a little of my background.

I come from an average family, with a younger brother. Since primary school I saw myself as a shy person, I do not talk much, especially in front of strangers and I think a lot. Even in polytechnic, sometimes my poly-mates would joke about me not speaking more than 5 words. In fact, they do not know that I was actually talking, talking a lot to myself... in my head.

Education was somewhat a breeze where I spent 5 years in Australia after my national service. I achieved two Master Degrees, one in IT specializing in Artificial Intelligence from RMIT, and another in E-Commerce from Deakin University. Though the degrees do not contribute to my career, as I am currently neither in the IT industry nor even close to it, my experiences in Australia during my study have, however, shaped me.

After graduating, I did not jump into the work force. Instead, I started as a freelancer, providing web design services. Thereafter I formed a partnership with a friend to market SingTel's corporate products, before finally venturing into direct selling in 2011, partnering with a public listed company, one of the leaders in the anti-aging industry.

Being in the Network Marketing industry is a fast track learning experience with more downs than ups. It is the personal growth that I have developed over the years that has kept me going. Till date, I have had the opportunity to facilitate business networking sessions for 20-30 attendees or more, conduct training and talks, speak on stage in front of hundreds, even thousands of people. It is definitely not easy... initially. While my head is always trying to reject the idea of doing things that are uncomfortable, most times fearful to me, my heart simply says:

"Take the Challenge! Just do it!"

This reminds me of myself making cold calls a couple of years back when I was marketing for SingTel as their Channel Partner. I kept thinking of what to say when the person on the other end picked up the phone. I even wrote myself a script. In the end, I gave up! I simply picked up the phone and dialed the numbers, even though my mind was racing fanatically, thinking of what to say next. The first couple of calls were not smooth. Eventually, I warmed up and it was not as hard as it seemed.

Yes! I'm an Introvert!

Nowadays, when I tell people that I am an introvert, it seems hard for them to believe, even for most of the introverts I have met during the Introvert Networking sessions. I believe it is because their perception of an introvert is somewhat different from the way I present myself in front of them. Unknowing to them, I am just like them, after any networking session, I will be mentally drained, and prefer to have a "Me Time" to re-charge myself over a cup of hot Chai Latte, working with my laptop in a nice, ambient environment.

Through observation and conversation with a number of my people, I found that an Introvert is being stereotyped as a person who is very quiet, shy, non-expressive, reactive, lacks confidence

93

and do not like to mix with people, especially strangers. Hmm....
This sounded like me in the past.

Networking with the Introverts

It was 3 years back, when I felt that I needed to expand my network
further, that I started to entertain the idea of attending other
business networking events, to meet up with strangers.

I started off my search via a website called Meetup. It is an online
platform that allows organisers to create meetup groups and events
for specific focus groups e.g., badminton, movies, even business
networking. In fact, I have heard a lot about it, yet was never ready
to venture into it.

While browsing through the website for meetup groups in
Singapore, I chanced upon an interesting group named 'Introverts
Networking Singapore'. It immediately caught my attention and I
joined the group with much curiosity, and attended their second
meetup session.

My first networking experience with the members in the introvert
group was somewhat relaxing. The objective of the group is simply
to get the introverts out to network. Thus, I did not have much
expectation then. To me, it felt like a sharing session without
personal agendas.

It was an afternoon session. There were only 9 of us seated in a
cosy room, around a long, rectangular table. Curtain was drawn
closed by request. My first thought was, "What's there to hide?"
And I realised that we just have different comfort level with the
public. My first networking session in that group, and the next few
that followed, were well hidden from sight, right within the Oromo
Café, located at the ground level of Shaw Tower.

Over years, the group has slowly grown to over 800 members for the Meetup.com Group[1] and over 400 from the Facebook Group[2], with an average turnout of between 10-20 introverts for our monthly networking sessions. In fact, we recently celebrated our 3rd anniversary with over 50 attendees.

Interestingly, when others heard of our Introvert Networking event, I have seen and heard of responses such as…

"How do the introverts network?"

"The event must be very quiet."

"Do the introvert talk to themselves during the networking?"

In case you are also wondering, the networking event is just like any other networking events. The only difference is that introverts take slightly longer time to warm up. However, when they get started, they are literally unstoppable!

My Changes

Comparing to myself from the past, there are definitely a lot of changes in terms of attitude and mindset.

From a person who does not talk much, to a person who can talk when needed, even speaking in public. Furthermore, I can be very enthusiastic when touching on my favorite topics related to Health and Marketing.

In the past, when I speak, my hands were down in fixed position. Nowadays, I notice that I'm more expressive with my tone, lots of hand gestures; I even feel confidence in my words.

---

[1] Introvert Meetup.com Group - http://www.meetup.com/networkingintroverts

[2] Introvert Network Facebook Group – http://www.facebook.com/groups/networkingintroverts

I am definitely more positive and grateful for the good and bad things that happen, because I believe

> *"Everything happens for a reason, a good reason*
> *that will make me a better person".*

Though I have changed, fundamentally I am still an introvert!

Introvert... Good or Bad?

Whether being an introvert is a good thing or bad, all lies in what we think. I chose to believe being an introvert is an advantage.

> *"What we think of, we're always right!"*

Whenever I hear people commenting they want to become an extrovert or they see introversion as a disability, I feel that they just lack the confidence and there is just too much negativity surrounding them to see things from a positive angle.

If only they experience what I had experienced, they will know it is never about introversion, it is all about our willingness to expand our comfort zone and make a decision to change.

> *"For things to change, I must first change".*

Like many other introverts, I too have similar traits. One of them is the tendency to over-think. There are times when I keep dwelling on negative thoughts and experiences, it magnifies and affects me emotionally, sometimes I need to sleep over it. Nowadays, I focus more on positive thoughts, it too magnifies and I feel fantastic and see things with a different light!

Same trait, yet different result. It's a matter of perspective.

Introvert and Public Speaking

An entrepreneur once asked me "Vern, as an introvert, how are you able to speak in public and even taking the role of an emcee?"

It has never crossed my mind that one day I will be speaking on the stage to a couple of hundreds, or even thousands, of people. However, I do know that I want to be inspired and be an inspiration to others. I do not know how, I do not know when. It is a seed planted in my subconscious mind since long time ago.

That little seed is then nourished by the sequence of events and my environment that bring out my innate potential through giving me the opportunity to grow myself as an emcee, trainer and a speaker. Ultimately, I must want it, allow it, before it can even happen.

Speaking in front of a crowd of strangers is different from presenting to your class mates. Like anyone else, I have a fear of public speaking and I cannot think straight when I'm nervous. When I'm nervous, I tend to speak louder.

My first foray in public speaking started from the Toastmasters Club. We had monthly chapter meetings, and each of us was being evaluated for our speeches based on project and themes. Over the years, I improved and expanded my comfort level of speaking in front of 10 to 20 people, sometimes more.

Later on, my involvement in BNI[3], one of the world's largest business referral organizations, gives me the platform to give a 60-second 'elevator' pitch every week to a group of business owners and entrepreneurs. On a rotational basis, I too have the chance to do a 10-minute showcase of my products and services. It was also with the support from my BNI members, that I conducted my very first 2-day 'Business Blogging Workshop'.

---

[3] BNI (Business Network International) - http://www.SingaporeBusinessReferralNetwork.com

In my current business platform, we have many meetings, and through my involvement, I am recognized for my strength and selected to be part of the emcee team. That is where I have more opportunity to develop myself in this role. Though nowadays, I am more experienced, I am however still nervous before going up on stage, even for just those 5 minutes.

The emcee role is crucial as I need to warm up the crowd within that short time period, so that the speaker will have a better chance to engage the audience. Furthermore, it is also a transfer and build-up of energy within the room.

Ironically, as an introvert, I myself also need time to warm up. One to two hours before the event, I will be practicing on stage with a microphone in hand, speaking as though I am in front of a full house audience. This works better for me than just practicing softly to myself. Most times I will need a small handwritten script in my hand, just in case.

Bottom line - the more I keep doing the same thing, the easier it becomes, the shorter my warm up time.

I am now more confident and can be ready anytime for action.

Introvert Striving in the Network Marketing Industry

I have never wanted a mundane 9 to 5 kind of life. Thus I ventured into entrepreneurship after graduating. By chance, I stepped into the Network Marketing industry in 2011. It started with just a decision to better my health for my kids through a 3-month weight management program, where I shed over 10kg and trimmed 4 inches off my waist. After that, I saw the opportunity and went on board full time wanting to transform my life and those around me.

Network Marketing, or MLM as some call it, is nothing new to me. In fact, being analytical and having been exposed to various industries through my participation in BNI (Business Network International), gives me the capability to better evaluate and understand the businesses platform.

It is a business so simple, that anyone can do it, yet it is not easy. However, to me, it is worth it!

There is only one key challenge in this business, and that is EMOTION. Emotion due to not having the results one expected, and emotion due to rejections. Many a time, we think too much due to lack of action, resulting in negative emotion and this creates a vicious cycle. That is why it is important to continuously immerse ourselves in a positive and supportive environment, especially amongst the successful people, because...

"You are the average of the five people
you spend the most time with."
- Jim Rohn.

In any businesses, finding the right mentor is important, their profile and their success should be relevant to us. And I am blessed to be in the right team, with a proven system and most importantly, mentored by a legend in the industry who is only in his early forties and happens to be an introvert too!

Because it is a low investment business that requires mainly time commitment, it is therefore easy for newbies to give up, and scramble back into their comfort zone. As entrepreneurs, we need a strong 'WHY' in order for us to persevere and succeed in this business. There could be so many challenges which may be our obstacles. They, however, could also be our motivator and a catalyst to our success.

This business is about building human relationships, and being introvert means we tend to be more thoughtful, sensitive and a good listener. Coupled with positive mindsets and massive action, that is all it takes to succeed in this business.

Outsiders may think that we are just selling products. Unknown to them, we are leveraging on the platform to fulfill our dreams, and that is something which most people probably would have forgotten in the midst of their busy-ness.

Gratitude

Every little step we take, every result we achieve, is due to a choice we made. And we have to be thankful and give gratitude in order to experience a positive emotion and aliveness! With that, I would like to end this chapter with 10 things I am grateful for:

1. I am grateful for all the challenges in my life, to make me a better person.

2. I am grateful to my wife and my parents for being supportive in what I do.

3. I am grateful for my 2 lovely kids, who are an inspiration to me.

4. I am grateful to be surrounded by positive, successful people.

5. I am grateful to partner with a company with a heart.

6. I am grateful to my business mentors who guided me with patience, and business partners who place their trust in me, to help transform their lives and those around them.

7. I am grateful to my BNI Chapter members and their support.

8. I am grateful for the opportunity to lead and to inspire as a leader.

9. I am grateful for all the people that make this book a realization.

10. I am grateful... Because I'm Introvert... I TRIUMPH!

BOUND, BUT UNBROKEN

Let not our minds be set
The folly of ancient thought
Had enslaved us all
To promises that Beauty brought
Lotus feet, bound and broken
Crippled the path we walked
It should not be this way
There was no price we could pay
Happiness could not be bought
All pain endured was for nought

Let not our minds be thus set
Frozen in time
It goes nowhere
The past is a trap
Move on with no regret
History, unkind
Must be left behind
Live as we wish
Not as others define
Theirs is not for us to follow
Ignorance, born and bred
Too wide a disease spread

Do not bend, do not bind
Let our feet grow
And take us where we want to go

Let our minds be free then
To do as we desire
Seek the moments of solitude
We so often require
Bound we may be by misperception
Unbroken are we in spirit
Though no flames we make
Feel the heat
A fire roars beneath
The quiet need not shout
The soft need not be loud
Every word
Unspoken will be heard
By results will be seen
Our powers from within

Names we have been called many
No offence need we take
A rose is just as sweet by any
And wallflowers do a bouquet make

~ Fiona Tan-Low

A BRIEF OVERVIEW OF
EXTRAVERSION AND INTROVERSION
ELIJAH LIM

The terms 'extraversion' and 'introversion' were used by the Swiss psychiatrist Carl G Jung to describe how people tend to be energized. 'Extroverts' tend to be energized by the outer world while 'introverts' tend to draw energy more from the inner world.

C. G. Jung applied the words extravert and introvert in a different manner than they are most often used in today's world. As they are popularly used, the term extraverted is understood to mean sociable or outgoing, while the term introverted is understood to mean shy or withdrawn. Jung, however, originally intended the words to have an entirely different meaning. He used the words to describe the preferred focus of one's energy on either the outer or the inner world.

Extraverts orient their energy to the outer world, while Introverts orient their energy to the inner world. One of Jung's and Isabel Myers' great contributions to the field of psychology is their observations that Introversion and Extraversion are both healthy variations in personality style.[1]

During World War II, two American women, Isabel Briggs Myers and her mother Katharine Cook Briggs, set out to find an easier way for people to use Jung's ideas in everyday life. They wanted people to be able to identify their psychological types without having to sift through Jung's academic theory.[2]

What emerged from the mother-daughter research was the Meyers-Briggs Type Indicator, or MBTI as it is popularly known. It has

---

[1]From http://www.myersbriggs.org/my-mbti-personality-type/mbti-basics/extravert-and-introvert.htm
[2]From http://www.myersbriggs.org/my-mbti-personality-type/mbti-basics/c-g-jungs-theory.htm

been said that personality or behavioural measuring instruments like the MBTI have caused people to label both themselves and others as being of one or other set of 'personality types'.

This is far from the truth.

Most 'personality' or 'behavioural' assessments are derived from frameworks which state quite clearly that what is being measured are 'preferences' and that there is no 'preference' which is to be preferred over another. Our 'preferences' are simply how we choose to express ourselves. Labelling either ourselves or others, casting ourselves and others into moulds, is because we as human beings have allowed ourselves to be dumbed down into thinking that our preferences are limitations. Few people actually bother to find out about tools like the MBTI, DISC, Tetramapping, Big Five, 'Strengths-based' assessments, 'Definitive Natural Abilities' or DNA assessments, and the like.

For those that do, it is still not easy to stay out of the rut of either judging others as being of a certain 'type' or of refraining from making any rational assessments at all.

We need to recognize that all of us dwell somewhere in between types, leaning towards one or the other. We also need to remember that humans are complex, intricately designed beings, and that attempts to define a human will fall short of satisfactory. Do not worry about 'using' the 'strengths' of whatever you think you have been told your style is. Rather, seek to use all that researched information to help you better understand others and how to best serve their needs.

You'll be so much happier and fulfilled for it.

ABOUT THE AUTHORS

Ashley Ella Choo

Ricardo Duran

Gary Guwe

Hazriq Idrus

Judy Koh

Vern Lai

Lee McKing

Elijah Lim

Kevin Phun

Esther Siah

Fiona Tan-Low

Mervin Yeo

Ashley Ella Choo
Senior Executive Search Consultant
Assistant Secretary General, 25th World
Memory Championships 2016

Ashley is in the business of talent acquisition and she takes personal responsibility to steward the profession.

She has always been passionate about referrals marketing. Working on both the agency and client side has allowed her to gain a detailed understanding of the power of referrals in shaping and influencing opinions and perceptions. She has always enjoyed the opportunity to share resources, connect people and encourage lifelong learning.

She is also the ambassador for the World Memory Championships 2016.

When she is not at work, she will be spending quality time with her God and her 3 children.

Connect with Ashley @

ashleyella.choo@gmail.com
fb.com/AshleyElla.Choo
linkedin.com/in/AshleyElla

Ricardo Duran
Customer Success Manager, APAC
LinkedIN Corporation

Ricardo Duran has lived in Japan, the United States, and Singapore. Living in various countries has allowed him to develop a curiosity in human behaviour among different cultures, especially from an introvert perspective.

As a Customer Success Manager at LinkedIn, he travels regionally and strives to provide solutions to the continuous challenges faced by the Human Resource industry.

Connect with Ricardo @

linkedin.com/in/RicardoNakasoneDuran

Gary Guwe
Serial-Entrepreneur & Award-Winning Speaker
Authoritative Art of Influence Coach

Gary is a serial-entrepreneur with business interests in education, IT & construction. An innate introvert, Gary realized his fear of public speaking and communication was holding him back at work and life, and set out to overcome his limitations.

Since mastering the skill, he has been headhunted and has worked with senior business leaders at various corporate organizations. He's also lectured post-graduate students at the National University of Singapore, then at age 27.

Gary continues to work with Small Business Owners, Corporate Leaders and Government agencies in areas relating to **Influential Communications, High Performance Sales, and Team Building**.

Till date, Gary has spoken to over 18,000 people in Singapore, Malaysia, Vietnam & Japan. His insights have also been sought by the media, having appeared on radio 938Live, The New Paper, The Straits Times, New Age Parent, AsiaOne and Lifehack.org.

Connect with Gary @

gary@catalyst-empowerment.com
www.Catalyst-Empowerment.com
fb.com/SuperInfluence
linkedin.com/in/GaryGuwe

Hazriq Idrus
Founder & Lead Consultant
The Speaking Factory Pte Ltd

Hazriq Idrus is an author and speaker on Business Creativity and Communications. Hazriq's mission is to empower professionals in achieving creativity, communications and team excellence through his signature theatre-based training programmes.

Tapping on his over 10 years of operational leadership, events management, corporate training, stage & TV acting experiences, Hazriq founded the theatre-based corporate training firm - The Speaking Factory Pte Ltd - to realise his mission. He believes that theatre-based training accelerates learning and also serves well as a tool for anyone who desires to add value to their well-being.

Besides speaking and training, Hazriq is also a dynamic master of ceremonies, facilitator, stage & television actor. Currently, Hazriq also lectures on Creativity as an Associate Lecturer at Ngee Ann Polytechnic. This book is his third under his belt after **'The Stage Fright Antidote!'** and **'Crowdsauce'**.

However, all of the above is nothing close when compared to the single production that he is most proud of – his only son, Rizzqi.

Connect with Hazriq @

hazriq@thespeakingfactory.com

www.TheSpeakingFactory.com

fb.com/Hazriq

linkedin.com/in/hazriq

Judy Koh
Principal Chef / Director
Caffe Pralet
Creative Culinaire The School Pte Ltd
(Singapore and Indonesia)

Judy Koh is the founder and executive chef of Creative Culinaire The School and Caffe Pralet. Together with her team of chefs, they cater at functions, supplying celebration cakes, pastries and dishes of different cuisines. They also conduct bakery, cooking classes, Professional Bakery courses and café running courses as well.

Judy is also the recipient of several awards such as the **World Guinness Book of Records** for Tallest Chocolate Sculpture and the **Singapore Book of Records** for Biggest Birthday Cake, Tallest Christmas Tree of Cupcakes, Longest Swiss Roll and Largest Cake Logo.

Happily remarried and blessed with a daughter, son and son-in-law who have joined the company, Judy looks forward to soar with them and her staff to greater heights. Their mission is to grow and prosper to be a blessing to others.

Connect with Judy @

judy@creativeculinaire.com
www.CreativeCulinaire.com.sg
fb.com/Judy.Koh.798

Vern Lai
Weight Management & Anti-Aging
Consultant
Certified Dr Sears Health Coach

Vern is in the business of transforming lives by helping people to achieve quality health and preserve their youth through the RIGHT supplements and personal care products that are 'All of the Good and None of the Bad'.

Having experienced effective weight loss and improvement in Psoriasis, an autoimmune disease, he strongly believes in the importance of the right nutrition and supplementations to maintain good health and beauty. And that is very lacking for most people.
He is an advocate for personal development and that has helped him in every aspect of life, from caring for his family to growing his team in business.

Vern is a father of two active kids who never fail to amaze and inspire him. He is also a fortunate man to have married a loving and supportive wife who complements him. They are his pillars of support that keep him anchored, yet allowing him to dream. Everything Vern does is dedicated to his family.

Other than linking up online via Facebook, feel free to invite him out during the day time for a chat over a nice hot chai tea latte.

Connect with Vern @

vernlai@gmail.com
fb.com/VernLai
linkedin.com/in/VernLai

Lee McKing
Hypnotist
Lee McKing Hypnotherapy Pte Ltd

Lee McKing is a certified NLP Master Practitioner and Conversational Hypnotherapist. The initial reason he learnt these skills was because he nearly died in his sleep and developed PTSD. After learning such skills, he resolved his own issues such as depression, anxieties and fears, as well as the PTSD.

McKing decided to help others just like him through a unique combination of NLP and Hypnosis. It has maximised the results in each session with his clients and it works amazingly well with his mission, to help people effectively.

McKing aims to re-educate Singaporeans and the world about the wonders of hypnosis and what it really means. With this in mind, he is now an author, a speaker and a hypnotist.

Connect with McKing @

mcking@leemcking.com.sg
www.LeeMcKing.com.sg
fb.com/LeeMcKing876
linkedin.com/in/LeeMcKing

Elijah Lim
Principal Consultant
Elijah Consulting Pte Ltd

Like the cygnet which thought it was a duckling, Elijah lived comfortably in the knowledge that he was an extrovert for some years after being introduced to concepts of behavioural science. Having lived so long in an environment where 'Just get it done!' was the daily commandment, he took such labels in stride even as he constantly mused on what they meant. The realization that his manifested behaviours actually tended more towards introversion didn't come in the form of a wake-up call, it was just another fact to be filed away and used where appropriate. His focus remained on lifelong character development.

He is known to emphasize Substance over Form. Other than that, contrary to popular belief, he does not drive a yellow school bus and is not a walking encyclopaedia.

Connect with Elijah @

elijah@elijahconsulting.com
www.ElijahConsulting.com
fb.com/ElijahConsulting
linkedin.com/today/author/ElijahLim

Kevin Phun
Lecturer, Practitioner and Speaker in
Responsible Tourism and Environmental
Sustainability

Kevin Phun is a lecturer, practitioner and occasional speaker in the area of Responsible Tourism and Environmental Sustainability. Kevin holds an MSc in Responsible Tourism from the **Leeds Metropolitan University**, and a 2nd Upper class honours in Bachelors in Tourism Studies obtained from the London Metropolitan University in the year 2000. He has been in the tourism and hospitality industry for about 15 years, being in a few sectors in the industry. He is also now pursuing his second Masters, an MSc in **Sustainable Development from the School of Oriental and African Studies**, University of London, U.K.

He has been teaching tourism since 2005, in various private education institutes. He also happens to be an occasional practitioner in Responsible Tourism. One of his recent projects is a position paper for Mandai Bird Sanctuary, a private bird farm here in Singapore.

Connect with Kevin @

 linkedin.com/in/Kevin-Phun-6ab38231

Esther Siah
Entrepreneur
Founder, The Card Room

Esther Siah is a self-taught card and craft designer. She likes to illustrate, design and create. The term that is widely used nowadays is 'Maker'.

Esther is widely versatile and highly innovative in creating anything beautiful, any craft she likes or that her clients require. She is therefore a de facto 'Maker-At-Large', and the handcraft market is so much better off for it.

She currently runs a handmade wedding & party invitation business which has been in operation for the past 10 years. The business slowed down over the last 2 years, as more people are exposed to DIYs, the materials for which have become increasingly easy and economical to procure. Ever resourceful, Esther stays ahead of the curve and now conducts workshops and meetup sessions to teach and share with people exactly how DIYs are done for their own parties.

When not crafting, Esther likes to go around scouting for nice places with good food (and coffee) to hang out, sometimes with friends, but mostly by herself.

Connect with Esther @

esther@thecardroom.com.sg
www.TheCardRoom.com.sg
fb.com/TheCardRoomFanpage

Fiona Tan-Low
Entrepreneur
Founder, Blue Moon Valley

Fiona is an infectiously cheerful person who lives Life at the incredible pace of a-laugh-a-minute.

A few years into semi-retirement, she keeps busy reconnecting with friends and family, and volunteers wholeheartedly in some community activities. Much of her time is devoted to her husband, children and grandchildren, and two adorable little furkids.

The strange hand of Fate led Fiona to found Blue Moon Valley, putting back to good use 30 years of administrative management experience and her hard-earned degree/diplomas from UK universities. Having endeared herself to her clientele and vendors, she is affectionately known to them as their Valley Godmother.

2015 proved to be a watershed for Fiona, during which time she re-examined her priorities and decided to return and concentrate on her first love, that of creative writing.

Connect with Fiona @

fiona@bluemoonvalley.com.sg
www.BlueMoonValley.com.sg
fb.com/BluemoonValley

Mervin Yeo
Networking Evangelist, Speaker, Author
MY Preferred Business Pte Ltd

As a Networking Evangelist, Mervin Yeo spreads the good news of networking through training, consulting, mentoring and writing. Hailed a 'Networking Guru' by a Straits Times reporter in 2003, Mervin has shown over ten thousand business owners and marketing professionals in Singapore, Indonesia, Malaysia and the Philippines a systematic and effective approach to purposeful networking and strategic referral marketing. A Certified Behavioural and Career Consultant, he has been interviewed on 938Live including The Living Room, Positive Business Minutes and A Slice of Life.

As an Introvert Leader, he runs the Introverts Network Singapore, a networking community for introverts in the marketplace which he started in May 2013. He plans to start similar networking platforms in Jakarta, Kuala Lumpur and other major cities in South-East Asia.

Connect with Mervin @

✉ mervin@MervinYeo.com
🏠 www.MervinYeo.com
f fb.com/MYnetworkingEvangelist

Thank you for being with us.

We hope you have enjoyed our stories,
as much as we have enjoyed sharing them.

It is our hope that, with more understanding
about introversion, you too will be encouraged
and inspired to discover and harness your strengths.

If you find values from within this book,
do let us know via our website

www.BecauseIAmIntrovert.com

~

Link up with the rest of the
Introvert community at

fb.com/BecauseIAmIntrovert

#BecauseIAmIntrovert

www.ingramcontent.com/pod-product-compliance
Lightning Source LLC
Chambersburg PA
CBHW070106070426
42448CB00038B/1784